The bushmen

For our parents,
Lady Pleasance Beadle and
Muriel and Stan Bannister

text
ALF WANNENBURGH
photography
PETER JOHNSON
ANTHONY BANNISTER

C. STRUIK PUBLISHERS

The bushmen

CONTENTS

C. Struik Publishers (Pty) Ltd, Oswald Pirow Street, Cape Town

First edition: 1979
Second Impression: 1984

Copyright photography © 1979 Anthony Bannister and Peter Johnson
Copyright text © 1979 Alf Wannenburgh

ISBN 0 86977 114 0

Designed by Walther Votteler, Cape Town
Photoset by McManus Bros (Pty) Ltd, Cape Town
Lithographic reproduction by Hirt and Carter (Pty) Ltd, Cape Town
Printed and bound by Tien Wah Press (Pte) Ltd., Singapore

ACKNOWLEDGEMENTS

While preparing the text of this volume the author was informed and guided in his research by many specialist publications on various aspects of the Bushmen by academic workers in the human sciences. He wishes to mention in particular Lorna Marshall's warm and comprehensive examination of the !Kung Bushmen in north-east Namibia, especially her fine study of !Kung religion; G. B. Silberbauer's pioneering survey of the /Gwi in central Botswana; and many papers by members of the Harvard Kalahari Research Group, of which Megan Biesele's studies of !Kung folklore and Richard Katz's insights into 'trance dancing' have been invaluable.

The photographers wish to thank sincerely the many organisations and people who helped in many ways to bring this book about. Foremost among these were: The Office of the President of the Republic of Botswana; South West Africa/Namibia Administration; the Director and staff of the Department of Wildlife, National Parks and Tourism of the Republic of Botswana; the Director and staff of Consolidated Diamond Mines Prospecting Limited; the General Manager and staff of Orapa Mine; the Department of Co-operation and Development of South West Africa/Namibia; the officers and men of the Botswana Police at Tshabong and Ghanzi; Major Coetzee, officers and men of Luhebu Military Base and the staff of Walvis Bay Radio Station.

'Of the many individuals who assisted us we are especially grateful to Ben Badenhorst, Maudanne Bannister, Isak Barnard, Ben Beytel, Dr K. Budack, Bushi, Alec Campbell, Sigi and Anne-Gret Eimbeck, Anthony Johnson, Clare Johnson, Oom Willi and Mrs Jonker, Herman and Annie Kühn, Tim Longdon, Tom and Wilma McGhee, Les Mamashela, John Marshall, Lorna Marshall, Charl and Janis Möller, Mark Muller, Barrie and Elaine Pryce, Johan and Ulna Steyn, O. P. Tebape, Adolf Waiderlich and Charles Williams. The assistance of Barbara Anderson with research and in establishing good communications with !Kung Bushmen in the field is gratefully acknowledged.

'But most of all we thank our many Bushmen friends for accepting us and our cameras among them, for allowing us to join them on their hunts and at their firesides, for their constant helpfulness, patience and infectious enthusiasm, and for the many happy memories we cherish. To Tishay, Bo, Dikau, Bau, Tsokhuma, Khu, Kaugi, Khunosha and Kumsau, our special thanks.'

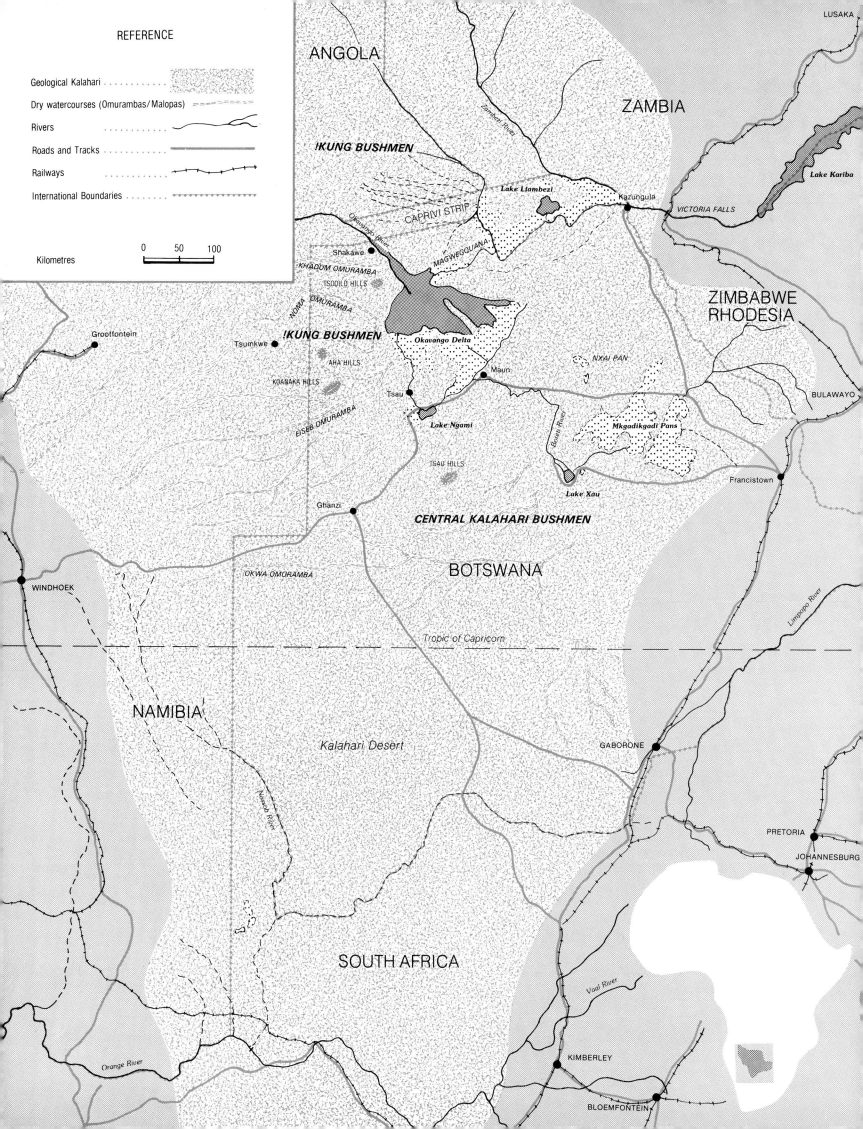

ANGOLA

ZAMBIA

LUSAKA

!KUNG BUSHMEN

Zambezi River

Lake Llambezi

Kazungula

VICTORIA FALLS

Lake Kariba

CAPRIVI STRIP

Okavango River

MAGWEGQUANA

Shakawe

KHADUM OMURAMBA

TSODILO HILLS

NOMA OMURAMBA

ZIMBABWE
RHODESIA

Grootfontein

Tsumkwe

!KUNG BUSHMEN

AHA HILLS

Okavango Delta

NXAI PAN

KOANAKA HILLS

Maun

Boteti River

BULAWAYO

EISEB OMURAMBA

Tsau

Lake Ngami

Mkgadikgadi Pans

TSAU HILLS

Lake Xau

Francistown

Ghanzi

CENTRAL KALAHARI BUSHMEN

WINDHOEK

OKWA OMURAMBA

BOTSWANA

Tropic of Capricorn

Limpopo River

NAMIBIA

Kalahari Desert

GABORONE

Nossob River

PRETORIA

JOHANNESBURG

SOUTH AFRICA

Vaal River

Orange River

KIMBERLEY

BLOEMFONTEIN

THE 10 000-YEAR GENERATION GAP

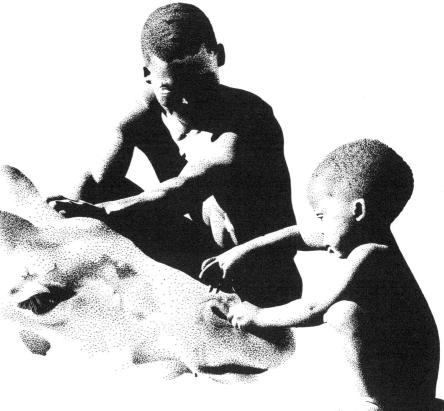

Compared with the great ages through which we chart the migrations of peoples and milestone their slow advances towards the 21st century, it does not seem to be so very long ago that the only human footprints in the soil of southern Africa were the impressions left around waterholes by the tiny feet of the people we call the Bushmen. But their isolation was invaded eventually when among the tracks of the little hunters appeared those of other men who came with flocks of fat-tailed sheep to drink at the waterholes. Still later came the black men, whose larger footprints were mingled with the impressions of cattle's hooves. And finally, the shod feet of men from another continent completed the obliteration of these smallest of footprints everywhere save in the thirstlands of the Kalahari, where even now the desert sands have begun to erase the last vestiges of the hunter.

And so, as we headed deep into the dry sandveld regions of Botswana and Namibia in our quest for the aboriginal southern African, we were conscious of the cosmic clock that rings out the changes for peoples and cultures, knowing that it was poised at the stroke of midnight for these men who lace their speech with clicks, aware that the chiming of the zero hour would be the death knell, not for the Bushmen themselves, but for the passing of the way of life they have led for thousands of years.

Informed estimates place the number of these distinctive people living in the Kalahari sandveld regions of Botswana, Namibia and southern Angola at upward of 55 000, but only a small percentage of them still live in the old way, dispersed in small hunting bands over the thirstlands. They are the survivors of the race of men who alone inhabited the entire subcontinent and much of East Africa many millennia before either the black men or the white men arrived, and they are among the last remnants of the world's hunting peoples.

From the time that manlike creatures first walked the earth some four million years ago, until peoples in the Near East began keeping animals and planting crops about 8 000 years BC, all mankind lived by the chase and on what they gathered of nature's produce. But ever since this agrarian revolution the number of people who sustain themselves by hunting and gathering has dwindled steadily. The isolation of the Bushman hunter postponed the start of his decline until only a few centuries ago, but the rate of his decline has accelerated to such an extent that any estimate of the number of Bushmen who still subsist in the old way seems like a fleeting figure on a digital counter running in reverse.

Fired by this knowledge, we came to the thirstlands as deeply interested individuals, to seize what was probably our last opportunity of witnessing a way of life that is perfect in its adaptation to raw nature. It is the way of men who have never tried to conquer their environment, who adopted instead the alternative of remaining an integral part of it. The rhythms of the traditional Bushmen are the rhythms of nature. The tempo of their lives fluctuates with its changes. It is integrated in their folklore, celebrated in their rituals and enshrined in their cosmology. All those thousands of years ago our own forefathers had chosen the path of conquest. In a sense, we wanted to experience the alternative they had foresaken.

On the Okavango River at Shakawe, about 30 kilometres south of where it flows from Caprivi into north-west Botswana, a district official had suggested we might find our unacculturated Bushmen at Gani. And so we set off optimistically one morning from the reed-wall enclosures and pole-and-grass huts of Shakawe, guided by an old Kgalagadi man carrying an antique shotgun held together with copper wire. Behind us faded the sounds of women doing their laundry in a quiet backwater, exchanging lusty banter with the fisher-men who paddled their dugout makoros among the papyrus and blue-flowered water-lilies, as we drove almost due west from the riverside town along a winding cattle path that wandered into and then followed the broad bottom of a shallow valley that was thickly wooded with thorn trees against the shimmering skyline on either side.

The proximity of the river conferred no benefit on the surrounding countryside beyond the distance for which its waters could be carried on the backs of man and beast. In an earlier age, when the trade winds blew further south than they do today and even more arid conditions prevailed in this part of the continent, this had been a true desert, and this valley had lain between parallel dune walls of bright red sand. But now, beyond the river's reach, it was a 'thirstland' rather than a desert. In a slightly more humid age, the run-off of rainwater from the dunes had deposited the finer material on the valley floor and leached the red iron oxide coating from the sand, turning it first yellow, then grey and eventually white. Thorn trees had taken root on the ridges and grass had spread over the valley.

Before the beginning of the last century, the only residents of this valley were Bushmen. The scarcity of surface water barred this region to the black people, who herded cattle and planted cereals. But the Bushmen husbanded no livestock and cultivated no crops. With their sharpened hardwood digging sticks they could obtain sufficient water for their own needs from the moisture that collected on top of an impervious calcrete layer a few metres beneath the surface of the sand. Their 'cattle', the gemsbok, kudu and eland they hunted, were as well adapted to the land and climate as were the people, and so too were the indigenous plants, whose fruits, leaves, bulbs and tubers the Bushmen gathered for food.

But eventually black people from the north found a way of making the valley suited to their way of life. They discovered that if they broke through the impervious layer with their iron tools, there were adequate supplies of water trapped beneath it to sustain their cattle. And so the non-Bushman population of the valley grew. The newcomers also hunted, but their ways were different. They frightened away the game, their cattle monopolised the pasture and laid waste many of the patches of natural plant foods. Much later, when central government was established, men and machines were sent to sink boreholes in the places where the sand overburden was too thick for the water to be reached with hand tools alone. The Bushmen found that the depleted natural resources of the valley were no longer hospitable to their ancient way of life. They had to readapt themselves, not only to a changed environment, but to the pervasive ways of other men, and they were thrown into increasing dependence on the crumbs that fell from the tables of the more recent arrivals.

The barbed branches of the thorn trees slashed at us as we passed through the valley, and every few kilometres we were obliged to stop and wait for the engine to cool. We caught occasional glimpses of brown cattle foraging in the parched grass for green shoots, herded by naked little black boys on donkeys. From time to time we drove close to a group of huts

or past a cattle pen corralled with cut and dried thorn bush, at the centre of which was a
primitive windlass, on which other small boys wound up buckets of water from a well below and tipped them into hollowed-out logs. And the oxen, in their frantic eagerness to drink, stirred up a heavy pall of dust over everything.

There were plenty of signs to forewarn us of the disappointment that lay ahead that day, but we were blind to them, believing that the unspoilt wilderness would suddenly open up ahead of us and that in it we should find our unacculturated Bushmen.

In the valley that morning, the first Bushmen we saw were a hunchback man and his young daughter who lived at our guide's cattle post. The man still wore the traditional Bushman apron of soft duiker skin, tucked between his legs and held fast behind in the cleft of his buttocks, but over it he wore a ragged shirt and a broad-brimmed black felt hat, and he was tending the calves in the thorned circle of his master's byre.

Under the supervisory eye of our guide's wife, the girl was pounding maize into meal with a wooden pestle as tall as herself in the shade of a lone camelthorn tree, and her vigorous movements revealed the classic lines of her people moulded in the thin cotton of her dress. These two had already accepted menial positions in another culture.

But our guide assured us that these were not the 'Masarwa' he had brought us all this way to see. He would take us presently to two large encampments nearby where the people still wore skins and hunted with bows and poisoned arrows.

Our pulses quickened as we approached the first of them and saw through a break in the trees at least a score of grass shelters in a large clearing thickly strewn with the golden orbs of woody monkey-orange shells and veiled in smoke from the embers of several fires. But as the people emerged from the shadows where they sheltered from the midday sun we sensed the aura of despair that emanated from this place. There was an odour of corruption here. It was not purely organic; this, in microcosm, was an ethos in decay. Here were men on crutches, babies infested with skin eruptions, young and old of both sexes with eye infections and displaying the symptoms of the fungal white hair sickness. Here were people, wearing every imaginable combination of cast-off modern clothing, trapped in a cultural vacuum by the irresistible historical forces that are driving them to bridge in a single lifespan all of mankind's great revolutions of the past 10 000 years, from the Stone to the Atomic Age. Surely no generation gap could be wider.

The second Bushman encampment our guide took us to that day was no better. Here even the customary grass shelters had been discarded in favour of huts in the style of the dwellings built by the Mbukushu who predominate in the valley nowadays. The larger size and darker pigmentation of many of the people here told of a long association between this band and the black cattlemen, betraying a cross-fertilisation that was not exclusively cultural. Disappointed, we were turning to leave and had already started moving towards our Land Rover, when suddenly we noticed an old man coming towards us through the tall grass on the fringe of the clearing.

Beside the other inhabitants of the encampment, he seemed to us at that moment to be so perfect that he could have been the incarnate spirit of the quintessential Bushman. Although the grey of his typically tufted hair disclosed his age, he moved over the ground swiftly and lightly, like an antelope, a natural grace articulating his delicately proportioned limbs and finely muscled body. His skin was a pale golden shade, and his dark eyes challenged ours, but without hostility. His bow had acquired a polished sheen through being constantly in his hands, and in the root-bark quiver slung over his shoulder were five reed-shafted arrows, each with a thick coating of poison.

'Do you still hunt?' we asked.

'Whenever I can,' was his reply.

And then, to explain further, he unslung his soft skin hunting bag and smoothed it out on the ground at his feet. Squatting beside it, he extracted five disks made of thick eland hide and heaped them in his left hand. Then, cupping them in both hands, he blew on them, touched them once to the ground and, shouting the word for 'fire', allowed them to spill out onto his hunting bag, snatching his hands back as they did so. He meditated on the disposition of the disks for a moment before gathering them up.

'I see no animals for me to hunt,' he said.

We had been told about these divining tablets, which may be made of hide or wood or bone, by a retired white hunter at a fishing camp on the Okavango River. He had respect for the Bushman's understanding of the wilderness and was in the habit of asking his Bushman tracker to 'throw his bones' on the eve of a hunt. He believed implicitly in their efficacy and told us of an incident to justify his faith.

'My client had a permit to shoot one jumbo,' he said. 'The night before the hunt my tracker threw his bones and told me that he could see two elephants. "No," I told him, "there must be only one elephant." But he insisted not only that there would be two, but that the chief game ranger, who was the scourge of poachers, would be there too. "This time you've slipped up very badly," I told him, because I was practically certain that the chief ranger was still away on long leave. Early next morning we picked up the tracks of a big bull and a cow. When we came to where only a thicket separated us from them, I sent my client on alone with the tracker, telling him that on no account was he to shoot more than one and that it had to be the bull. I waited in my truck and some time later I heard two shots. At the same moment I saw the chief ranger's Land Rover coming up behind me in my rear-view mirror. As he reached me, the Bushman ran up and said that the client had wounded the bull with his first shot and killed the cow with his second. The ranger dashed off into the bush with his rifle, and after a few minutes there was another shot. The ranger got the bull. There *were* two elephants. The bones are never wrong.'

In that clearing on the ridge of a fossil sand dune at Gani we told the old man about our quest and asked him where we should go. Once more he stacked the eland hide disks, blew on them, touched the earth and tipped them on to his flattened hunting bag, crying out *'da'*.

But this time he took longer to interpret the pattern in which they had fallen. He sat on his heels, pointing first to one disk, then another, tracing their oracular relationship in the air above them with a finger, clucking to himself in an undertone.

'The *xusi* speak of earth,' he said finally. 'I see earth in three mounds that are taller than many trees.'

All the people there watched us drive away, but the old man's eyes seemed to reach out and touch us.

THE EARTH
IN WAITING

Many Bushmen have spent their entire lives in the Kalahari without ever seeing a mountain or even a large hill, for it is only in a few places that the bedrock breaks through the vast expanses of flat sandveld. One of these places is the Tsodilo Hills in north-west Botswana. The highest of the hills, Mount Male, thrusts the tip of its quartzite cone more than 300 metres above the surrounding plain. Close beside it a cluster of lower hills enclosing a depression combine to form Mount Female. Two kilometres away stands the small solitary hill called Mount Piccanin, 'the little one'.

Were these hills, we wondered, the 'three mounds of earth taller than many trees' the old man at Gani had spoken of?

We arrived at the Hills less than an hour after the Little Rains made their first call of the season. Approaching slowly through soft sand from the north-east, we watched a cloud darting snake-tongued lightning at the summit of Mount Male. In the valley between the two larger hills the wet leaves of the knobthorn, combretum, tamboti and marula trees glittered like festive tinsel and the smooth bark of the young baobabs diffused the late-afternoon sun on their polished highlights. It had been only the briefest of showers and the leaves soon lost their added adornment, but the magic of that first moment of the Little Rains lingered on long after the fragrance of damp earth, so redolent of the African veld after rain, had been carried away by the breezes and when all that remained were the dry pockmarks left by raindrops in the sand.

The season of the Little Rains, as some Kalahari Bushmen call it, is for most of them a time of promise as well as privation. It is not a season fixed by the calendar but comes when the first raindrops touch the earth after several months of drought; months during which the Bushmen have lived through a season of ice-blue days and frosted dawns, followed by the hottest season, spent under a glaring sky, upon searing sand.

The Little Rains may arrive at any time from October to December. Meanwhile the heat continues. High winds gust over the burnt grasslands, and dust-devils, which the Bushmen say are the restless spirits of people who took their own lives, dance in the yellow and grey landscape. The dormant earth awaits the heavy showers that will come early in the new year to restock the natural larder of the animals and people who depend on it for sustenance.

The showers that come with the Little Rains are too scattered and meagre to relieve the drought, and this is usually the time of greatest hardship for the Bushmen. Those of them who have permanent water sources cannot wander far from them, even though most of the plant foods in the vicinity have withered or been exhausted. Those living in the central Kalahari, where there is no permanent water, find that the wild tsama melons from which they obtained most of their moisture in the earlier dry months have shrivelled and vanished, while the new growth of gemsbok melons has yet to appear. Now they must dig deep in the sand with their pointed sticks for the surviving fibrous tubers that have become their only remaining source of moisture.

But the Bushmen see no sense in cursing the rigours of the season. What foolishness to complain because something is what it is in the nature of things. If the Big Rains came early, surely the next dry season would be too long to endure? And all around them the earth heralds the approach of the rainy season, beginning to release its promise of another cycle of reproduction and growth: the trees are suddenly greener; the grass, drained of its colour and brittle from the drought, puts out bright new shoots; flowers appear overnight; and the surface of the earth is transformed, as if by magic.

This environment is often harsh with the Bushmen, taxing to extreme limits their understanding of its ways and the ways of all that live in it. But it rewards their patiently acquired understanding by granting them the rudiments of their subsistence from one day to the next. Historically, it has protected them from others, enabling them to survive here as a unique branch of humanity, long after the Bushmen who formerly occupied lusher regions have disappeared under and before the advance of more purposeful peoples.

We found ourselves in the Bushman encampment at the foot of Mount Male's sheer western slope unexpectedly. One moment we were crawling along the winding track between the hills; the next moment we had blundered into the middle of their camp before we even realised it was there.

Grass huts were strung out across a sandy clearing, in the centre of which, encircled by lively children, a woman was shaving another's head with a blade held deftly between thumb and forefinger. The carcass of a young gemsbok shot the previous day hung limply over the angle of a camelthorn tree, its flayed flesh and muscle encrusted with turquoise flies, and in an unshaded spot on the ground an old man was staking out its hide for curing, driving in small wooden pegs around the edges with the clubbed head of his axe.

The stone ramparts of Mount Male, flushed by the effulgence of the lowering sun, rose from a fringe of small trees and bushes behind the camp. We were reassured by the sight of springhare hooks dangling their long, flexible shafts from the tops of shade trees in the clearing. Here, indeed, were people who had not abandoned their traditional arts of survival.

Suddenly we were surrounded by Bushmen. The children stopped playing, the men and women left their tasks, and all came to look at us and discuss us among themselves. But when our eyes intercepted a curious stare, there was embarrassment, laughter and something else. Then the old man who had been pegging out the hide shook our hands, grasping first the palm and then the thumb, and greeted us with a word: 'Tobacco?'

Fortunately, we had with us a good supply of the coarse leaf tobacco that is known colloquially as 'sheep lick', because it also serves that purpose. We handed over a large packet and tubular bone pipes were stuffed there and then, lit and passed from mouth to mouth until everyone, including the small children, had drawn in a few lungfuls. Some of them drew so deeply, and the smoke disappeared inside them for so long, that we half expected to see it suddenly pouring from their ears. They were all laughing and talking together now as the pipes did their rounds. We sensed the first tentative communication between these Bushmen and ourselves.

When finally the pipes were stuck upright in the sand to cool, we left to set up our own camp, telling them that we would be back next morning. Our arrival had broken their tobacco famine, and for a Bushman there is nothing worse than being without tobacco.

These were the Bushmen whom expeditions under François Balsan and Laurens van der Post had failed to locate when they came in the 1950s to examine the profusion of paintings that make the Tsodilo Hills the great rock art gallery of the thirstlands.

There are hundreds of paintings on exposed rock surfaces at more than 20 sites in the Hills. These red ochre figures of animals, some in silhouette, others in outline and the best of them delicately shaded, are in places accompanied by the small handprints of Bushmen in the same pigment or by white schematic designs that are thought to be the more recent work of non-Bushman doodlers. Together they represent five different styles and belong to at least three of the periods into which the rock art of southern Africa has been classified. As far north as Tanzania and as far south as the Cape Province of South Africa paintings have been found that bear a strong resemblance to some of the pictures we saw at the Hills. There are similarities between certain of them and later style paintings on the walls of granite caves in Zimbabwe-Rhodesia which strongly suggest that the Tsodilo Hills are the link between them and the later development of this style in the rock art of Namibia. In fact some specialists believe that the Hills lie on an old east-west migration route used by Bushmen fleeing the central Zimbabwe-Rhodesia plateau after powerful black pastoralists from the north began flooding into their country over 1 000 years ago.

Archaeologists do not yet have a reliable way of dating paintings on exposed rock faces. While some of the paintings at the Tsodilo Hills appear to be fairly recent, there are others, sometimes underlying later, clearer pictures, that are very indistinct and possibly very old.

Quartz artefacts and potsherds found beneath ancient rockfalls in certain of the caves indicate that the Tsodilo Hills have indeed been inhabited for a considerable length of time. Numerous huge scars left by massive cliff-face collapses raise the possibility that entire areas of much older paintings may have been destroyed and that those that survive are only the tail-end of an artistic tradition of great antiquity that has died out here, as it has throughout Africa, for today there are no living Bushman rock artists.

A few evenings later we climbed 20 metres up the western side of Mount Female to a narrow ledge backed by an imposing slab of rock on which the best pictures at the Hills are painted. From here we could see distant clouds sprinkling the first of the Little Rains on far-off places, as the sun dipped towards the land behind them. And then, at the very instant when the flat thornveld below turned suddenly black in the horizon's shadow, the rock behind us looked as if it were radiating immense heat, glowing yellow as a furnace fire-brick, and for a few moments the dull red ochre of the painted eland and giraffe and the tiny handprints of long dead Bushmen had the lustre of molten scarlet wax. We scrambled down quickly to level ground, for darkness followed swiftly and was as total as the old Bushmen's abandonment of their art.

Why those little people of long ago painted, and why they gave up painting, are today largely matters of conjecture, for they left no record of their reasons in the oral traditions of their descendants, and present-day Bushmen do not even associate their forefathers with the paintings. But the vast number of paintings and engravings left on the rocks at over 6 000 sites in southern Africa are testimony at least to the exuberance of the artists in their graphic celebration of nature, which was refined by them over many centuries until it reached its greatest perfection just as more powerful strangers, black and white, began occupying their ancient hunting grounds. Their subsequent paintings reflect the increasing fragmentation of their way of life and finally cease altogether with its eclipse in the areas dominated by the immigrants.

Old /Gao, who had been pegging out the gemsbok hide the afternoon we arrived, knew more about the Tsodilo Hills than any of the other Bushmen. At about 70 he was very old in a society where a man may reckon on a lifespan of 45 years. His body was webbed with deep wrinkles, so tightly packed that they overlapped one another in folds of loose skin which had been blackened by a lifetime of sleeping naked, curled around the embers of open fires.

Neighbouring Bushman bands recognised him as the traditional 'owner' of the territory adjoining the Hills, for he had inherited from his father an exclusive claim to the resources of the vicinity, and it was from him that his band derived their food-gathering rights. But, although his age assured him of their respect and affection, his nominal 'ownership' invested him with no authority over them, for the Bushman social order is based not on authority, but on agreement and subtle communal sanctions.

We had been there a few weeks when, as we sat beside his fire with the rest of his band one evening, old /Gao began telling us the story of the Tsodilo Hills. He was sitting on his haunches in front of his hut, fondling his small son and occasionally dropping a twig on to the coals to light the faces of his audience.

'Long ago, when the world was different and things happened which no longer happen today, this big hill that you see here was a man,' he said, pointing over his shoulder towards Mount Male. 'This hill was a man who had two wives, but the trouble was that he loved the second woman more than the first and gave his attentions only to her, and this was the cause of a quarrel between the first woman and her husband. It grew into such a fight that eventually the woman took a heavy stick and hit her husband over the head, giving him a deep wound, which can be seen to this day. Then she threw down their youngest child, whom she had been carrying, and ran away. Her older children followed after her, but they could not persuade her to return to her husband, and she ran even further away to the west. When she reached that far-off place, which we do not know, she built her own hut and lived alone.

'After some time, the Great God, ǂGao!na, saw that she was alone in this far-off place, and so he went to the man and asked him what had become of his wife. The man told him that there had been a terrible fight and showed him the scar on his face, where she had hit him, and the place where she had thrown down their child. ǂGao!na then said that, as there was no peace among them as human beings, it would be best for everyone if he turned them all to stone. And so, the man became this big hill, as you know, and the first woman became the little hill that stands on its own, while the second woman and all the children became the group of hills in the middle.'

Old /Gao dropped another twig onto the coals and waited for it to flare. 'That is the story of Tsodilo that I heard from my father and my forefathers,' he said. 'If you like, tomorrow I shall take you to see the scar on the man's face and the place where the child was thrown down.'

What did he know about the paintings, we asked.

'The person who did those paintings is not known to us,' he replied. 'My father and forefathers did not have any stories about them. They found them there as you see them now. I think the paintings must always have been there.'

We asked him what he knew about the origins of the Bushmen.

'The story that I heard from my father, who heard it from his father, is that we Bushmen came from the west,' old /Gao said. 'After the Great God made them they were in a very good place in the west, the name of which my father never told me. But soon after they were created, there were wars which forced my forefathers to leave that nice place of theirs and seek other places of rest. They wandered until they found this place, and eventually I was born and found that I was at Tsodilo. That is all I know about where we Bushmen came from.'

Old /Gao's story told us nothing about the origins or general history of the Bushmen as a branch of humanity, but it contained all he knew about the origins of his own band, and it seemed to him that the earliest acts of his ancestors that he had heard about must surely

have been committed very soon after ≠Gao!na, the Great God, had created them. Of the
wanderings of his earlier ancestors and others of their kind during all the thousands of years that preceded the wars that had driven his own people to make the only migration they remembered, he knew nothing at all, and did not even suspect that they had existed.

Except in so far as they feature in the history of other peoples, the Bushmen are people without history. For countless generations they have lived in small hunting bands, isolated within their territories from all but a few neighbouring bands, practising a way of life that remained unchanged for thousands of years, in a world where the only changes were seasonal and the seasons themselves were part of an unchanging annual cycle. Anthropologists call such a form of existence 'stereotyped' and describe such societies as 'non-progressive', but both are really only other ways of saying that they have achieved a way of life that harmonises the limits of their environment so perfectly with what they conceive their needs to be that they have no reason to want to change it. Their concerns are the cares of the present. There are no dreams of national glory to colour their future and no mighty rulers or generals to milestone their past. An old man may recall a particularly severe drought that occurred in his own lifetime, and the feats of a renowned hunter may be recounted by his grandchildren, but after they bury their dead they do not return to visit the graves. Beyond memory, history quickly shades into mythology.

From an academic point of view, old /Gao's story about the origin of the Tsodilo Hills is mythology, while his account of how his band came to be living there is history. But the !Kung Bushmen, among whom old /Gao's band is numbered, do not make this distinction; to them, both stories are about real people and tell of actual events. The people of their mythological stories are not regarded as being the same as present-day Bushmen, however. They are people of the 'early race', and the events related are believed to have taken place in a very remote age, when all the animals were people and things happened which could not possibly happen today. That was when the Great God still lived among the 'early race' on earth. But the mythical era ended when he gave these 'people' their individual animal forms, moulding them in the 'fire of creation', branding them with their distinctive animal markings. Since that time, animals have been animals and men have been men, and ≠Gao!na has lived in the sky and been divine.

Ever since the first Europeans settled in southern Africa towards the middle of the 17th century, the question of the Bushman's origins has intrigued a host of romanticists as well as serious scientists, chiefly because they differ so conspicuously in appearance from the negroes, who are the dominant physical type south of the Sahara. Where the latter are usually tall, solidly built and dark brown to black in complexion, the Bushmen seldom grow to more than 155 centimetres and are lightly boned and lean muscled, while the colour of their skins tends towards yellow. Certain physical peculiarities of the Bushmen, such as the skin folds in their upper eyelids and the tendency of some women to develop pronounced accumulations of fat over their buttocks, have been used to support fanciful theories of exotic origin. But in more recent years the anatomist, geneticist and comparative linguist have joined the anthropologist and pre-historian in finding an answer to this question, and although there is still learned controversy over some of the details, it is now generally agreed that the Bushmen evolved in Africa and nowhere else, and that they and the black men probably come from the same root stock. Geneticists have also found evidence which suggests that evolutionary changes undergone by the black men have distanced them more from the original people of Africa, while the Bushmen have changed least and remain closest to the prototype of all Africa's indigenous peoples.

What we knew of this aspect of the Bushmen's prehistory deepened our appreciation of the time we spent with them, colouring our experience with the sensation that we had somehow travelled backwards through time into aboriginal Africa.

From the first night we rolled out our beds in the entrance of a cave about two kilometres from the encampment of old /Gao's band. There we were woken each morning at first light by a swarm of bees that droned out of the knobthorn thicket opposite and passed low over us like a squadron of bomber aircraft as they flew into the cave to find damp rock surfaces at which they could slake their thirst. Generally not long afterwards, two of the Bushmen, Gumtsa and ≠Owe, would emerge from a footpath through the same thicket to accompany us back to their camp.

Gumtsa was the most worldly of these Bushmen. He alone of all the men in the band had been to a great modern city and worked deep in the earth beneath it in what seemed to us the most unlikely place for a man accustomed to the wide open spaces of the Kalahari. While visiting Shakawe to barter skins for salt he had been recruited to work in the gold mines on the Witwatersrand. But, as he put it, 'I always kept my skin'. When he returned from the mines he packed away his European clothes, adjusted his duiker skin loin flap and resumed the life of a hunter. The smattering of other languages he brought back with him equipped him better than any of the others for handling relations with visitors like ourselves. The golden undertone and delicate proportions of his body reminded us of the old man at Gani whose divining tablets had brought us to this place. Although he was one of the younger men in the band, he appeared quite naturally to take the lead in their joint activities. And yet, he had not been born into the band but had entered it by marrying Xama, daughter of Khan//a and his wife //In, and was the father of a teenage daughter named !Ungka.

≠Owe was similar in build and complexion to Gumtsa, but was more a follower than a leader, and he was usually quite content to remain behind and keep an eye on our camp while we went off somewhere with the other men.

There were 17 members of the band, including three youths, a teenage girl and four small children, and the gemsbok carcass hanging in the camelthorn tree at the Bushman camp shrank rapidly. Shared as meat customarily is between all the members of the band, big chunks of it disappeared each day into three-legged iron pots over cooking fires around the camp, and soon there was nothing left save the horns and hooves. Even the bones had been cracked and the marrow extracted.

But before the last of the gemsbok was eaten its hide was completely dried out by sun and desert air. Old /Gao removed the wooden pegs that held it to the ground and placed the stiff hide in the shade of a tree near his hut. With a small, sharp adze he then set about removing all the dried flakes of flesh and connective tissue that still stuck to its inner surface. He worked on it in the relative cool of late afternoon, kneeling beside it and scraping away at it in short, vigorous bursts, in between which he rocked back onto his heels and honed the cutting edge with his knife, rubbing the two briskly together and periodically raising the adze edge to his lips and whistling over it to gauge its keenness. All the scrapings from the hide were carefully collected and kept, to be added later to the contents of his cooking pot.

It was little acts of this kind that emphasised for us how integral the conservation of resources is to the Bushman way of life. But it does not arise out of their conscious regard for some ecological abstraction. It is a habit conditioned by many centuries of adaptation to an environment that is seldom generous, usually niggardly and often critically tight-fisted.

While we were out hunting with Gumtsa one day he found a wild asparagus plant. He uncovered the bulb gently and removed the sand around it with his hand to give us a better view of it. Then he covered it up again carefully. When we asked why he had not put it in his bag to take it home with him, he replied that it was still 'a child' and that he would come back later for it when it was fully grown.

We noticed that the Bushmen's way of making the most of what is available without spoiling the source extends even to the conservation of their own body energy. Although they have no sets of tables for balancing their energy expenditure against their food intake, they nevertheless realise that, in the hot dry seasons particularly, every little bit of energy they conserve extends the length of time for which their food resources will suffice. Before embarking on any project, therefore, they first consider whether the reward will justify the effort.

There was consequently little activity in their camp during the middle hours of the day at that time of year. While the sun was high they sat about in the entrances of their huts or in small groups in the straggled shadows cast by their shade trees, talking, cracking nuts, threading beads or strengthening a bow by binding it with sinews taken from the neck muscles of the gemsbok. Sometimes old /Gao's eldest son would take his thumb piano from the tree outside his hut and thrum a few tunes, or some of the children would sing in reed-thin voices. Heavy work, like collecting firewood or fetching water, was left for the early morning and late afternoon.

We were returning from an unsuccessful hunt on another occasion, when a small steenbok broke cover ahead of us. Old /Gao and Gumtsa's father-in-law soon lost interest in the chase and retired to some shade, but Gumtsa remained in the hunt. The steenbok was apparently unwilling to flee beyond the borders of an area in which some patches of tall grass and scrub offered it a little concealment. And so it bounded off, first in one direction, then another, crossing and recrossing its own trail several times. Often it vanished completely, until Gumtsa's Bushman eye spotted it immobile behind a clump of grass or screened by the branch of a sapling, its broad ears cocked and open to every sound. Each time this happened, Gumtsa went into a stalking stoop and tried to get closer to it in short little runs that were more like dance steps, his bow held in front of him, the poisoned arrow already nocked. He tried to keep downwind, approaching it in a wide semicircle, but there was no wind to speak of; only a gentle eddying of air that carried sounds and scents in all directions. Whenever he came close to being within bowshot of it, the little steenbok somehow got wind of him and leapt off again, its head high, its rufous flanks glistening, its slender legs skimming over obstructions.

The steenbok, which is among antelope what the Bushman is among men, and so like him too in grace of movement and capacity for surviving on roots and tubers for food and water, was tiring. It seemed to us to be only a matter of time. But the Bushman, because he is a man of nature, is also subject to its balancing limitations. He does not hunt with the advantages of packaged food, wheeled transport and powerful rifles. Nature treats the Bushman hunter and his quarry alike. Both are equally nourished by it. When one is weakened through hunger and thirst, the other generally is too. And so Gumtsa was also tiring. Quite abruptly, he straightened up, returned the arrow to his quiver and began walking back to where we were waiting.

Why had he given up, we wanted to know, particularly now, when they were so short of meat? He pointed to the sun, which was already past the middle of its ascent, saying that it was now too hot and that such small game would not provide enough meat to recompense the effort. He was not exhausted, but he had abandoned the pursuit when he realised that inevitably he would be if he continued, and the steenbok had more than an even chance of eluding him anyway.

The two older Bushmen did not bother to ask his reason. They had assessed their chances differently from the start, and so had waited in the shade for Gumtsa's exertions to end, as they knew they would end. On our way back, however, they made a short detour to gather some plants, which would not in themselves have been considered worth coming all this way to collect, and which probably they would have ignored had there been meat from the hunt.

One did not take more from the land than one needed, because then there might not be enough of it when it was needed. But, as we were in the vicinity and it would require no more than a few minutes to collect all they wanted, it was better to do so than go home empty-handed.

Beside our campfire that night, we decided on reflection that Gumtsa probably realised as clearly as the older men that the steenbok would get away, but that he persisted in order to please us, to share with us the experience of the hunt that he knew we wanted to share.

This willingness, even eagerness, to please was the quality that most endeared these Bushmen to us. The moment they understood what we wanted, they hastened to oblige, and they did so with zest and obvious enjoyment. They observed our behaviour closely, and no doubt discussed it around their communal fire. And so precise were their observations, which were sharpened by their habit of studying and decoding the behaviour of every animal that shared their habitat, that more often than not they anticipated our wishes. It was an uncanny feeling. Sometimes we felt like strange animals that had blundered into their territory; a source of food to be hunted with the tender skills of diplomacy and care.

To suggest that their solicitude was not entirely altruistic does not mean that it was insincere. Most human relationships are based on an exchange of some sort, whether it be of affection, service or something material. But our transactions with the Bushmen were not grasping or commercial. The terms of exchange were never mentioned. They simply knew that we would contribute to their needs if they included us in their activities. That they could give us their time without any loss to themselves was crucial to their way of life. It was the only basis on which mutual good-feeling could develop.

The Tsodilo Hills Bushmen are better off at this time of year than many other bands. They are not reduced to dependence on melons or tubers for their water supply. Thanks to abnormally heavy rains during the previous wet season, there were still two seeps at the foot of Mount Male, about a kilometre from their camp. In the evenings, when the hills are suffused by a salmon shade and the men gathering firewood cast long shadows, the women, balancing clay pots, gourds and ostrich-egg shells on their heads, go in a silhouette procession to the nearest seep. There, one by one, they crawl into a vertical cleft in the rock and with dried monkey orange shells scoop clear water from a tiny pool.

Even in bad years, when the seeps dry up before the new rains come, there is still the eternal spring on top of Mount Female. Some years they are forced to live for a while on top of the hill to be near this water supply, but they prefer not to stay up there during the hot months, because this is when snakes are most prevalent among the rocks. In the daytime the deadly cobra and mamba can be avoided by someone with a trained eye and a knowledge of their habits, but at night, when the snakes hunt, the Bushmen have no defence against the silent serpentine invasion of their camp. The bite is as lethal as a poisoned arrow. The Bushmen have no antidote. Old /Gao could recall only two years in which the spring on top of the hill had dried up completely. Those years, he said, they moved to the west 'to drink milk with the Damara'.

Permanent water from the seeps gives the Tsodilo Hills Bushmen greater mobility, enabling them to range more widely in search of food without fear of becoming dehydrated, and thus they are in a position to conserve more of their supplies of tsi beans (*Tylosema esculenta*) and mongongo nuts (*Ricinodendron rautanenii*) for far longer than would otherwise be possible. They also sometimes barter skins for dried maize and sorghum at an Mbukushu cattle post a few kilometres from their camp, and our presence had contributed a few sacks of maize meal, a quantity of rock salt and a couple of kilos of dark leaf tobacco. What they most lack, however, is meat protein. They feel it in their bodies. Animals are scarce in this season. The young gemsbok had been a windfall, but now it was finished. The steenbok was the only game animal seen since then, and it had eluded them.

Early one morning, Gumtsa arrived at our cave to say that they wanted to go springhare
hunting. The place where they were most likely to find them was too distant for them to go
there on foot, considering the size of a springhare. But its flesh was particularly esteemed,
and if we could take them closer to this place in our Land Rover, it would be worthwhile.

From the moment we first caught sight of the springhare hooks in the Bushman camp we
had been hoping for a chance to see them in use. Nowadays the actual hooks are fashioned
from scrap iron, but their slender shafts, up to six metres long, are still made in the
traditional way from several flexible sticks, scarfed at the joints, stuck together with a dark
mastic and tightly bound with sinews or bark fibre. According to old /Gao, the very first
springhare hook was made by the Great God himself, who was angry with the springhare
for borrowing his son's skin apron to dance in and not returning it. To punish the springhare
he devised the hook to make its flesh accessible to men.

We picked up Gumtsa's father-in-law and ≠Owe at the camp and set off, with Gumtsa
perched on the bonnet to show us the way. He directed us to stop in what seemed to be the
middle of a thinly grassed sand flat, dotted with bushes and occasional thorn trees and
rimmed with thick bush. But the dense surround proved to be an illusion. After walking for a
while, we noticed that we never seemed to get any closer to it. It was only an impression
created by the spaces between distant bushes and trees being filled visually by yet more
distant bushes and trees.

By this time our Land Rover had disappeared from view and we had doubts whether we
would be able to find it again without Bushman assistance. There were only the sun and the
outline of the hills in the east to give us orientation, and although they would have enabled
us to find our way back to camp, we had no idea in what relation they stood to the position
of our vehicle. It was swallowed up in the illusion of thick bush somewhere behind us. If we
paused and looked around, we could pick out several distinct scenes, individual groupings
of trees and bushes, but, as we moved, our perspective of them was continually changing,
and so there were no fixed configurations to serve us as landmarks.

The three Bushmen, on the other hand, seemed to be familiar with every plant and its
position. They walked side by side ahead of us, their hooks thrust through their waistbands,
the long shafts trailing behind them. They moved at a steady pace that was neither fast nor
slow. If we stopped to examine something we had to run to catch up afterwards. Occasionally, one of them would bend to scoop a handful of black berries from a low shrub in
passing. These are too few and scattered to be collected for taking home, but they are
valuable sustenance for the hunter in the field, who cannot encumber himself by carrying
food.

We passed several places where the sand was churned up by the entrances to springhare
burrows, but the Bushmen gave them scarcely a glance. They could tell that they were
uninhabited.

We hung back a little at first, thinking that our heavy bodies and boots would alert their
quarry to our approach. But Gumtsa said that it made no difference, because it was the
springhare's natural defence of remaining concealed underground when danger
approached that made it easy to catch them with the hooks.

These animals only move about in search of food and water at night. During the day they
remain in their warrens, which have several entrances, and in which they are safe from
most predators, but not from the Bushman. If they were to leave their burrows at the hunter's
approach, they could easily escape with erratic kangaroo-like leaps of several metres,
outdistancing the fleetest pursuer. But instead they burrow deeper and hope that they will
not be noticed. But it is a vain hope when they are up against the keen-eyed Bushmen and
they quickly fall prey to the hooks.

After a while the three Bushmen found what they were looking for: fresh tracks, left by a springhare while foraging the previous night, that would lead them to the hole in which it was presently hiding. Following such a trail is not easy. The tracks are several metres apart and do not follow a straight course. The Bushmen discussed the trail among themselves as they walked. They would point out to one another a scratch mark in the sand that would indicate a point of landing and take-off between one leap and the next, and the depth and angle of the imprint, together with the direction in which the disturbed sand had been thrown, would reveal to them the distance and direction of the next landing and take-off point.

The Bushmen could read these signs at a distance of a few metres, while we could find them only if we watched to see where the Bushmen pointed and then examined the ground there closely. Sometimes they amounted to no more than a bent grass blade or a few displaced grains of sand.

The trail led eventually to a warren with entrance and exit tunnels covering a fairly large area. Here the Bushmen spread out and began scrutinising the sand at the mouths of the tunnels for signs of present occupation. When one of them found a hole that looked likely he inserted his hook and began plunging it deeper into the burrow with each thrust in a kind of stoking action, pausing between thrusts occasionally to place his ear against the shaft and listen for sounds of movement underground.

They tried several holes in this way without success. When we thought we knew the signs they were looking for, we began examining entrances ourselves. Finding marks outside one of them, we called to Gumtsa's father-in-law, who happened to be nearest. But he merely glanced from a distance at what we were pointing to and said: 'That was yesterday.'

He was the one, however, who found the first springhare a few minutes later. The moment he detected the tell-tale vibrations through the shaft, he began plunging the hook deeper with rapid movements to get it under the hare and so prevent it from burrowing deeper. He lost it the first time, but the other two immediately thrust their hooks into tunnels they judged were connected with the first to drive it back, and a moment later Gumtsa's father-in-law called out that he had it on his hook. He then sat down and leant back slightly to exert a constant pull on the shaft, less than a metre of which was still above ground.

Gumtsa immediately dropped his own hook and began digging with an iron hoe over the spot where, judging by the length of the shaft that was buried, the impaled springhare should be. The hole he dug was big enough for him to squat in and was more than a metre deep before he exposed the animal's ears. He then removed the sand around it with one hand, holding the ears firmly with the other, freed it from the hook and held it up for us to see. It was already dead. The hook had penetrated its chest, which was torn and bloody. He then took a short length of vine from his hunting bag and tied the two front paws together at the first joint. Then he placed it stomach down on the ground and systematically broke all the bones in its body with blows from the back of his hoe, starting with the front legs, working his way down the spine, splitting the pelvis with a heavier blow and finally shattering both back legs, which were then entwined like folded arms or half a reef knot.

The springhare contributed very little to the protein requirements of the band, but we saw its turkey-brown flesh in the cooking pots that evening, and there was satisfaction on the faces of those who later sat around the fire sucking its bones.

The next time the divining tablets were thrown they would tell of the heavy rains to come. Meanwhile, the Bushmen could but wait. They had only three poisoned arrows left between them, and they would not be able to obtain fresh poison until after the rains. Meanwhile, three more kills were the most they could hope for, if each of their arrows found its mark.

It was in times like these, old /Gao told us, that they used this prayer:

Help me. See me. I am hungry.
See that I am sending my children into the bush.
Let them find an animal.
If not a living animal then at least a dead one
Which they can pick up and carry home,
So that I and my family can live for a day.

THE WATERS OF RESURRECTION

The season of the Big Rains is when the potential of the Little Rains is released. From January to March is a period of resurrection and rebirth. This is when nature throws the 'bones' which presage whether it will be a good year for plants and animals and men. It is the time when grey leaves freshen and plant foods begin to ripen and, if the rains are good, when pans, pools and waterholes brim.

The now extinct Cape Bushmen used to tell many tales about the power of water to resurrect. In one of them, after an ostrich has been killed and eaten by Bushmen, some of its blood-stained feathers are blown into a pool of water and there grow again into a whole ostrich, the very one that was dead and is now alive again.

In another story, the mythical Mantis, in his human character as one of the 'early race', finds that his grandson has been killed by baboons, who are playing a ball game with the child's eye. Mantis joins in the game and, gaining possession of the eye, places it in a pond, where it once more becomes the complete child, the grandson whom the baboons had killed.

These old Bushmen of the Cape directed some of their prayers to the moon, for they believed that it was Moon who controlled the rain. And Rain they considered to be a supernatural personage, who sometimes appeared as a black bull.

In terms of their conception of nature, Rain was to be shown respect, because he came armed with thunderbolts to chastise those who offend him, and girls were the objects of his special attention. Thus women did not walk about in the rain, lest the lightning seek out their scent. If a shower caught them in the open, they took care whenever the lightning flashed to look immediately at the place where it had struck, believing that in this way they were able to turn back the thunderbolts aimed at them and that Rain would then pass them harmlessly by. It is said that girls killed by lightning were taken away to become stars, or be the wives of Water as the flowers that grow in pools.

They also believed that the clouds are the hair of people who have died. This notion has an echo in a story still told today by Bushmen of the central Kalahari about their mythological trickster, G//awama who bears some resemblance to Mantis of the south. In this story, he is bitten by a python near the present town of Gobabis, in Namibia. With his leg immobilised by the inflammation, and in the grip of fever and raging thirst, G//awama tries to cross the Kalahari to drink at the waters of Lake Xau, dragging his swollen leg behind him and scouring out the valley of the dry Okwa River in the process. But the Okwa ends in the

central Kalahari. According to one ending to this story, G//awama is at this point so
refreshed by the scent of the distant Boteti River that he is able to walk the rest of the way. Another version is that G//awama does not reach Lake Xau. He dies where the Okwa ends, his body putrifies and becomes the water of rivers, and his hair flies up into the sky and becomes black rain clouds.

These Bushmen see Rain as a giant leopard with lightning flashing in its eyes and thunder rumbling in its throat, an animal to be tamed with flattery, so that the rain may fall and the desert blossom, so that there may be water and food for the animals and people.

Old /Gao's band at the Tsodilo Hills, like other !Kung Bushmen of the north-west, distinguish between gentle Female Rain and violent Male Rain, which must be shown due deference, for he cuts the haughty down to size; indeed, it is the tallest trees that are blasted by lightning in the flatlands.

They tell several regional variants of a story concerning the way in which men first learnt about water. It involves the beautiful Antbear Girl, daughter-in-law of ≠Goa!na, who, in a way that is explained by the fact that these things happened long ago when things happened which no longer happen today, was also the wife of Elephant.

In the story, Elephant alone has knowledge of water, which he keeps from his wife and her people so that he can have it all for himself. But his secret is betrayed by mud caked on his legs when he returns from the waterhole. Still he refuses to share the water with them, and in the ensuing quarrel he is killed by his wife's brothers, the little black birds called 'the children of the rain'.

The Bushman preoccupation with rain and water is understandable. There are very few inhabited places that are as long without standing water as parts of the Kalahari. The prospect of dying of thirst is remote from the thoughts of urban man, who needs only to reach out for the nearest tap to slake it. But Bushmen cannot take water for granted.

Those who live in north-western Botswana and neighbouring areas in Namibia generally have year-round access to limited supplies of standing water, but in vast areas of the central Kalahari there is no permanent water, and no standing water at all for nine or ten months of the year. After heavy rains, a little may collect and remain for a few days in the hollows of pans and in impervious depressions in ancient riverbeds, but during the long dry months the Bushmen who live here must obtain their moisture from other sources. They may conserve some in ostrich eggshells, but not enough to last them any length of time.

The hollows in some trees hold water for a while. Sipwells, at which underground water may with effort be sucked up through a hollow reed, can sustain a hunting or gathering party in the field. But for most of the year they must depend for water upon melons and tubers and liquids squeezed from the rumen of their prey.

As the Bushmen in their natural state live on the produce of the unimproved veld, with neither the technology to build dams and sink boreholes, nor the means to cultivate crops and keep livestock, the amount and distribution of the rain that falls and the capacity of the earth for retaining it are critical. Rain is vital to them, not only as the ultimate source of their own water requirements, but also because it determines the growth of the plants on which they and the animals they hunt rely for food. Without rain there would be only dry desert air and barren sand.

Rainfall in the Kalahari varies considerably from one locality to another and from one year to the next. In the northern parts of this region the annual rainfall is usually between 35 and 40 centimetres. In the central and southern parts mean annual totals are between 25 and 35 centimetres, but the variation from year to year is so great that the actual rainfall received in any one year may be anything from five to 45 centimetres. And often there are several bad years in a row.

The landlocked position of the Kalahari at the centre of the subcontinent and its general elevation of more than 1 000 metres, combined with the prevalence of warm, dry northerly and north-westerly winds, reduce it to aridity for most of the year. But, for a few months in summer, north-easterly winds bring in masses of tropical air that has passed over the humid lowlands on Africa's distant Indian Ocean coast. At any time in this season of the Big Rains the clouds which gather in the morning may swell into thunderheads by early afternoon. Then the eyes of the giant leopard flash and a mighty roar bursts from its throat, the swirling winds are lashed to gale force and the clouds empty themselves over the land.

In these storms as much as eight centimetres of rain may fall in less than an hour, but the Bushmen know that it may be many days before another storm visits the area, and it can also be the only rain they receive for a year.

The first of the Big Rains had not yet come to the Tsodilo Hills when we awoke one morning and found Gumtsa inspecting the interior of our cave. Had we, he asked, considered what our situation would be like after a heavy shower. Had we noticed that the labyrinth behind us had several openings to the sky through which the run-off from the rocks above would drain. Did we realise that we had unrolled our beds in what, for at least a few hours after a thunderstorm, would be the path of a stream. Even in the first chamber there was a depression which had filled with water during the little shower that had fallen on the day of our arrival, and although it had drained away completely, there were water marks that showed clearly where it had overflowed and run halfway to where we slept before being absorbed by the sandy floor of the cave.

We were aware of this but had done nothing about it because we did not intend remaining at the Hills into the wet season. There were other bands of Bushmen whom we wanted to visit on the border with Namibia and deep in the central Kalahari, and we knew that we would have to leave before the rains turned the roads into mud slides, deep pools and quagmires. But, knowing that Bushmen can forecast rain from insect and plant behaviour, we listened to what Gumtsa said and, although we did not envisage staying there for more than another week, we agreed to his suggestion that they build us a hut.

All Bushmen who have not been influenced by the styles of other peoples build their shelters on roughly similar lines, but the care and effort they put into construction and durability depend on the pattern which locality and season impose on their lives. If these conditions permit them to remain in one place for a length of time, their huts are sturdy and well made, but if they must be continually on the move, the shelters they erect are often no more than a few branches lightly grassed to serve as a windbreak, much like the tiny play huts that Bushman children make for themselves in crude imitation of their elders. The huts of the Tsodilo Hills Bushmen were of the strong and durable kind, and it was one of this type that they proposed to build for us.

The next morning the whole band, with the exception of old /Gao, his wife and some of the smaller children, filed out of the thicket opposite our cave, bringing with them their implements and sufficient water to last them the day.

The site we chose for the hut in a small clearing in the thicket was rejected with little more than a glance by Gumtsa, and it was only after our next light shower, when we saw the thousands of winged termites swarming out of the ground in that clearing, that we understood why it was unsuitable. The men discussed various prospects among themselves and finally decided on a level area at the foot of a cliff that was not too far for convenience from our camp kitchen.

The widow N!ai took the other women off to cut grass, while the men began preparing the ground. Gumtsa described a large circle in the sand with his toe and marked it off at intervals of slightly more than a third of a metre. They all then sat down to dig at these points, first loosening the soil with their sticks, and then, with their forearms held vertical, removing the sand with the tips of their outstretched fingers, excavating gradually deeper

until they had scooped out holes that afforded an arm a tight fit up to the elbow. When the
holes were all completed, the men went off to cut the equivalent number of long, tapered branches of similar thickness and flexibility.

Meanwhile, the line of women returned with large sheaves of grass balanced on their heads, like a classical study of reapers coming home from the fields. They stacked the grass on one side and then sat in the shadow of the cliff to rest and crack open the ripe monkey oranges they had plucked along the way, using twigs to fork into their mouths portions of the delicious fruit, with its savour of bananas and mangoes and something sour. They were still relaxing happily in this way when the men reappeared with their branches and joined in eagerly.

They passed around a few pipes and chatted among themselves, but eventually they ran out of topics to joke about, their inactivity began to pall, and they began drifting back to their tasks. The women left to cut more grass and the men started fitting the thick ends of the branches into the prepared holes, turning them so that their natural curves inclined inwards, and compacting the sand around the buried ends with their feet. They then cut long, pliable wands and moulded them to the perimeter in equally-spaced horizontal courses from just above the ground to waist height, binding them tightly to the uprights wherever they intersected, using bark stripped from a knobthorn tree as twine. These wands give rigidity to the structure so that its shape is not distorted when the tips of the uprights are arched towards the centre and bound together. Once the basic shape of the hut is firmly established in this way, the horizontal coursing of thin branches is continued to the top and completes what looks like a big dome-shaped cage.

By this time the women had returned with their last loads of grass, and they immediately set to work tying small bundles of the grass to the framework, packing it so that it hung in dense layers, with each successive layer overlapping the one beneath it to ensure that the outer surface would shed the rain.

All this was done in an atmosphere of thorough enjoyment, as if they were all taking part in a communal game. There was much laughter when Gumtsa began tying the wooden lintel into place over the entrance and then sneaked a look at us over his shoulder and raised the lintel higher before securing it. But it was only when the last bundle of grass was tied into place, the fringe of grass over the entrance trimmed with a knife and the outer surface of the dome criss-crossed with a network of knotted strips of bark, that we realised that this hut was larger than the ones they built for themselves; that it had in fact been tailored to our size.

It was a fine hut when it was finished, and it could have served us through a long stay, but we slept only three nights with its fresh-cut fragrance in our nostrils. And then the rains came, accompanied by all the violence of a tropical deluge; water ran from the mouth of the cave, as Gumtsa had forecast.

We took our leave of the Tsodilo Hills and their Bushmen the following day and headed back to Shakawe to find out the state of the roads that could lead us to other Bushmen in different environments.

The caprices of the weather may cause some temporary changes in local conditions, but there are also permanent differences between regions due to varying combinations of climate and topography. These are responsible for the differing vegetation patterns, the number and kind of animals that can survive in a region, and the ways in which its Bushman inhabitants have had to adapt to its peculiarities in order to survive on what is available to them.

Probably the chief reason why the Kalahari is not a sterile waste of exposed sand is the extremely fine-grained texture of the sand itself which, instead of permitting the rainfall to drain away to great depths, absorbs and holds it near the surface, where it enables vegetation to survive long periods of drought. Small variations in relief, localised differences in soil consistency and occurrences of rock outcrops and calcrete deposits, all play a part in creating a patchwork of shrub, bush, tree and grass savanna.

In the north-west, the range of the !Kung Bushmen is a region of some 84 000 square kilometres, bounded by the Okavango River in the north and east, by the Ghanzi farming areas in the south and the Namibian escarpment in the west. It is a transitional zone of tree and bush savanna, lying between the dry shrub savanna to the south and the lusher vegetation of the river and the unique inland delta of swamps where the Okavango waters disperse into a maze of channels and eventually percolate into the desert sands. It is a region ribbed with fossil sand dunes and etched with dry river beds, and ancient watercourses that once flowed eastwards from Namibia where the Herero tribesmen call them *omurambas,* to the Okavango, where they are called *molapos.* Here, although the major rivers carry underground water at all times, the only permanent standing water throughout the year is found in the large circular pans that occur in the ancient watercourses that formerly drained eastward into the Okavango. The smaller pans in the *molapos* hold water for shorter periods of anything from a day to a few months after receiving rain.

The central Kalahari region, which is roamed by bands of /Gwi, Nharo and other Bushmen, is a mosaic of vegetation types, in which a relatively small range of plant species combine in different proportions to produce areas of scrubland, thornveld, grassland and bush and tree savanna.

In the northern part of this region, the Big Rains arrive a little earlier and depart a little later than further south. The soil is slightly richer and dunes that have been stabilised by vegetation give wind protection to thickets of camelthorn, purple-pod terminalia, sickle bush and hookthorn with a dense undergrowth of grasses, creepers and various shrubs, such as the white bauhinia, the brandybush, donkey berry and Kalahari sand raisin.

Southward the dunes level into an expanse of featureless sand, thinly covered with grass and small shrubs and dotted with occasional pans and clumps of trees. Still further south this gives way to scrub woodlands of stunted camelthorn, blue thorn, bastard umbrella thorn, buffalo-thorn, leadwood, silver terminalia, the rain tree and the shepherd's tree. To the east they are joined by mopane, monkey orange and red syringa, and large areas are covered with mixed thickets that include the trumpet thorn and the poison-grub commiphora, on which the *Diamphidia* beetle feeds, and beneath which the Bushmen dig for the beetle's grubs, which they use to poison their arrows. Rolling dunes in the extreme south-west are sparsely covered with isolated clumps of grass and an occasional grey camelthorn, hookthorn or shepherd's tree growing on a crest.

Because of their knowledge of plants and animals and their perfection of the subtle skills that enable them to survive under these harsh conditions, the Bushmen are thought of today typically as desert-dwellers. The hard fatty accumulations over the buttocks of some women of child-bearing age and older have been regarded as a specific biological adaptation to desert conditions, something akin to the camel's hump, which makes it possible for the women to suckle their young through times of drought and famine. But there is no strong evidence to support this belief. There is in fact nothing to show that the Bushmen are in any respect biologically adapted to their thirstland environment. Their responses to its demands are cultural; through their skills, knowledge and flexibility in adapting to its challenges they have acquired the art of understanding it and living with it. Cave paintings show that the women displayed this characteristic when there still were Bushmen living in lusher habitats and that they occupied every type of environment, from the Cape to the Zambezi and further north up the East African coast for thousands of years before Europe 'discovered' southern Africa.

The disappearance of the Bushmen from the more verdant regions they previously

occupied has, on the other hand, led to a reverse line of argument that the Bushmen who
survive in the thirstlands today are descendants of those who abandoned their more kindly hunting grounds to better-armed white and black invaders and fled to refuge in the Kalahari. But the art of living in so exacting an environment could not have been acquired all of a sudden. Here a refugee with no knowledge of the plants and water sources of the alien territory in which he finds himself will quickly die of thirst or slowly starve to death. It is an art refined through countless generations that perhaps encompassed the period of climatic change that compelled each successive generation to adapt a little more to a habitat that was gradually becoming more arid. The Bushmen in the lusher regions were eliminated by war, foreign diseases and cultural and biological assimilation by other peoples. The forefathers of the Bushmen living in the Kalahari today no doubt occupied the thirstlands for many centuries, probably for several millennia.

The early history of these people, their movement and migrations, how they came to be where they are now, the points at which their pasts converge, are still a puzzle for which scientists offer tentative, and often incompatible solutions. Among people so few in number and so physically alike, all of them living within a single geographical region, one might expect to find traces of historical connections, a shared mythology and related languages. But research and enquiry have cast little light on their past associations, there is wide divergence in the mythological contexts within which they account for the natural order, and they speak not only a bewildering variety of dialects and mutually unintelligible languages, but linguists tell us that these languages actually belong to several unrelated language types.

None of the numerous researches has yet given much insight into the connections between the different groups of people who speak these many tongues, all of whom we commonly call Bushmen. But the problem of deciding whether the /Gwi and Nharo hunter-gatherers living in the central Kalahari are Bushmen speaking Hottentot languages or Hottentots living as Bushmen is only a matter for academic dispute. They are in terms of their material culture and the manner of their subsistence as much Bushmen as are the !Kung of the north-west and the !Xo of the south.

This is not to say that their way of life is identical in every particular. They inhabit dissimilar environments that require them to make different adjustments. To the extent that the territories they occupy differ, so too do they. But what they do share is a state of mind, a common attitude towards their habitat, a similar approach to its demands and the ability to fit into it unobtrusively.

In recent years, academics have attempted to replace the name 'Bushmen', which they feel is pejorative, with 'San', which is the appellation, meaning 'gatherer', that they were given by the old Cape Hottentots. But this is a nicety that never concerned the Bushmen themselves. In none of their languages did they have a single name for all the people whom we generally call Bushmen or San. Before other people impinged on their territories they were not even aware that other men existed from whom they should distinguish themselves. There were only people and animals, who had also once been people. They had a term for the people of their own band, and another for the members of neighbouring bands with whom they had familial or visiting relationships. All others, Bushmen and non-Bushmen, were simply strangers.

Concepts such as tribe, race and nation are foreign to their thinking. Indeed, when they speak of such divisions today, they use the imperfectly understood terminology they have learnt from the languages of people who deal in such abstractions. Thus, when we asked old /Gao at the Tsodilo Hills to tell us about the origins of the Bushmen, he spoke only about his own band.

The notions of band and territory exist only in relation to one another; if there is no band in a locality it cannot be called a territory, and without a territory there can be no band. Every Bushman band has a territory in which its exclusive gathering rights are traditionally recognised by other Bushmen, although the origin of the tradition may long ago have been forgotten. While the borders between adjacent territories may be defined by natural features in the landscape, the actual shape and size of each territory are determined by its internal resources, for it must include adequate sources of water and food to sustain human life through all the seasons. The quantities in which it is capable of supplying these minimum requirements is a natural limitation on the size of the band that occupies the territory. If the number exceeds the capacity, the survival of the whole band is placed in jeopardy.

The smallness of these bands, which usually comprise from 40 to 60 people of all ages, and their relative isolation from one another have been suggested as possible reasons for the large number of dialects spoken, and, because the Bushmen have lived in this way for a considerable length of time, may also account for the differences between their languages and even explain the divergence of what are presently still regarded as discrete language types.

Although many of the smaller details of life may vary from one band to the next, according to the peculiarities of their respective territories, it is nevertheless possible to generalise to some extent about the broader differences between the life patterns of the larger linguistic groups, which are also rooted chiefly in environmental variation.

For us, that first trip to the Tsodilo Hills became several trips undertaken at different times of year to a number of places in Botswana and north-eastern Namibia, before we were able to make comparisons.

The most obvious differences between Bushmen occupying dissimilar regions appear to stem from the various ways in which they obtain water.

In the north-western Kalahari, where there are many permanent waterholes, but where vegetable sources of water such as the tsama and other melons are scarce, we found that a band can only exist independently if its territory includes a perennial water point, at which the band camps for about six months of the year when there is no water elsewhere in the veld. Here they remain from the time that the last temporary pools dry up until the return of the Big Rains, when they break up into smaller groups to range freely over their territory or visit friends in neighbouring bands.

While we were at the Tsodilo Hills, old /Gao's two unmarried sons rode off on a pair of donkeys the very morning after the first of the Big Rains to visit another band some 80 kilometres away, where they hoped to find brides. Gumtsa's father-in-law was planning to go with his family to visit a relative in the Khaudum Valley, stopping to eat at some plant food colonies he knew of on the way.

In the central Kalahari, on the other hand, we found that, apart from Bushmen who have access to borehole water, bands do not remain in one place during the dry season. Indeed, as they are without permanent standing water, they could not survive in one place at this time of year, when they rely almost entirely on the tsama and gemsbok melons for water. Throughout the dry months they shift about continually, from one patch of melons to another, eating the food plants that grow in association with them in different localities. It has been estimated that each Bushman eats about five kilograms of melon a day to obtain sufficient liquid. Towards the end of the dry season, when there are no longer any melons, each requires the moisture of about 20 tubers, which must be dug from the ground with considerable effort, under conditions which result in moisture loss through sweat of about three litres a day.

Although Bushmen are generally envisaged in the more romatic role of hunters, it is their plant gathering activities that provide their food base. Apart from furnishing some central

Kalahari bands with as much as 90 per cent of their water, plants also contribute anything
from 60 per cent to over 80 per cent of the food consumed annually by Bushmen.

Bushmen could survive without meat, but without their plant food resources they could not. It is easier to gather than to hunt, and also more reliable. Animals may move away in lean times, but the plants are indigenous to the locality, adapted to dry conditions, and so never fail completely. With their knowledge of plants and their uses, Bushmen are able to provide for almost all their needs; building materials, weapons, tools, twine, glue and soft-toned musical instruments.

A wide range of edible roots, bulbs, berries, fruits, melons, nuts and wild leaf vegetables are available, but as several are usually in season at the same time, some may be eaten only occasionally, for the Bushmen naturally indulge their preferences when they can and concentrate on the more appetising of the plant foods that may be gathered in any given season. Depending on their locality, the Bushmen in the north have either the mongongo nut or the tsi bean, both richer in protein than the soya bean, as a staple that provides as much as half their total diet. Bushmen living further south have no single most important food and rely on more than a dozen different species to make up their staple diet.

Everywhere the Big Rains usher in a time of plenty for the Bushmen. Game becomes more numerous and, within a few weeks of the first rains, the ripening of the *Ochna* and *Grewia* berries heralds the richest season for these people. The presence of temporary surface water in most areas liberates the !Kung in the north from their long confinement to their waterholes and they disperse in small family groups over their territories to where the hunting is good and where their favourite plant foods grow. Towards the end of the season, when there is still water to be found in the hollow trunks and root systems of trees on the dune crests, they come together again in larger groups, to enjoy the fruit of the mongongo and gather its new crop of nuts that will be their mainstay in the months that lie ahead. In the central Kalahari the Big Rains reunite the small groups of Bushmen who dispersed during the dry season, and for two or three months they are able to wander from one temporary waterhole to another and revel in the luxury of standing water.

This is also occasion for gratifying another time-honoured Bushman passion, for this is the honey season.

Bees are not generally plentiful in this dry land, but their honey is highly esteemed by the !Kung, who accord it illustrious status by giving the name 'Mother of the Bees' to the wife of the Great God who created all things.

In the season of the Big Rains, men and women are continually on the look-out for hives. As the sun set we often observed them pause to see in which direction a bee flew, because they know that at this time they fly straight back to their hives. When they find a hive they smoke out the bees and remove the honey, but if the hive is not yet ready for opening, the finder will mark it and return later for the honey. This is truly a case of 'finders keepers' for if another comes and removes the honey from a marked hive his crime is regarded as being worthy of death.

George Stow, writing about the old Cape Bushmen during the middle of the last century, says: 'A beehive of this kind in the mountains when once discovered became the sacred property of the finder. Woe to the man who carried off the honey from a marked hive, which was usually distinguished by stones heaped up before it as a beacon. There have been instances where such an encroachment was punished with death.'

The Rev. John Campbell of the London Missionary Society, who in 1813 journeyed through parts of the Cape still inhabited at the time by Bushmen, wrote that 'Bushmen over the whole country lay claim to all the honey in the mountains as their property. They mark the hives in the rocks, as farmers mark their sheep; and should they find, on their regular visits, that any hive has been robbed, they are sure to carry off the first cow or sheep they meet. They say that [other peoples] have cows and sheep that live upon the grass of the land; that they have none, wherefore they have a right to the bees who live only on the flowers.'

Campbell added that most people found it more prudent to recognise this right and purchase honey from the Bushmen instead.

In the later years of the century, when only a few remnants of the Bushmen were still clinging to the land of their fathers, says Stow, 'they still returned each year to their old haunts to open the hives'. And long after the Bushmen themselves had disappeared from these areas, the sharpened hardwood pegs they had driven into the faces of precipices to reach the hives and the small heaps of stones with which they had sealed their ownership remained as evidence that this land had once been theirs.

While out hunting with parties of men, it was not uncommon for us to see one of them dig up a root and put it in his hunting bag or collect a sheaf of leaf-stemmed plants and attach them to the end of his digging stick so that he could carry them home over his shoulder, but this was only casual gathering and never the main purpose of the outing.

Although men sometimes assist, gathering is the chief task of the women, and one which places them in the position of being the principal providers of food. The edible plants a woman gathers are not shared between all the members of the band, as meat is, but it is her responsibility to gather sufficient to feed herself, her family and perhaps an ailing or aged relative who is unable to gather. If all the women do their work, everyone will eat. If any woman is lazy in this regard, she is likely to meet with the strong and open disapproval of the whole band. 'Who does she think she is?' they will ask one another loudly with the intention of being overheard. The band cannot afford to carry passengers, nor can she resist their disapproval for long.

But in our experience all the gathering expeditions were jolly events. With the Bushman's gift for converting chores into social occasions, they often had something of the atmosphere of a picnic outing with the children.

These were usually one-day affairs for which several women formed a gathering party. Women do not go out singly to gather, we were told, because apparently a 'fate worse than death' awaits them in the bush in the form of a lusty legendary baboon who waits to waylay any woman he finds wandering about on her own.

The women take with them on these expeditions their sharpened hardwood digging sticks and a supply of water in ostrich egg shells, which they carry in nets made from cords of twisted sinews. They have skin bags for conveying smaller quantities of plants they gather back to camp, and the traditional kaross, fashioned from a whole gemsbok hide, is fastened around the body in such a way that it provides two large compartments, in which loads of up to 25 kilograms may be carried home at the end of a day's gathering.

Small children who need to be carried are an added burden for the women, but they almost always accompany their mothers, and when they grow a little and are able to walk the whole way themselves, they become useful assistants. These expeditions are in fact a 'school of life' for the children. Here they learn to be observant and acquire the detailed knowledge of plants that is essential for their survival. By their teens they know the typical habitats of most of their food plants and can identify each of them in all its seasonal manifestations. With eyes thus trained they remember the precise locality of an individual plant and are able to find it again, even though it is situated many kilometres from their camp and its presence is indicated by no more than a few centimetres of dry stalk. This remarkable development of visual memory also enables them to find their way in an environment that seems featureless to other people. They navigate by mental maps on which they imprint the relationships between the various plant communities they pass through.

While we were camped near Tsumkwe in north-eastern Namibia, we were interested in
identifying the ingredients of a powdered herbal mixture that the women rubbed into their skins for fragrance.

Tsamgao, one of the local Bushmen who acted as our interpreter, consulted the women and was then able to give us the names of all but one of the herbs used. We asked him to find us a specimen that we could have identified.

Next morning he arrived at our camp with his highly pregnant wife, //Kushay, whom he said knew where some of these plants grew.

We followed //Kushay for about five kilometres among tall stands of worm-cure albizia and leadwood, the sacred ancestor tree of the Hereros, and low thickets of candle-pod acacia, through interleading glades of waist-high grass, in which occasional rain trees and true fan palms seemed to offer landmarks, but which in retrospect were indistinguishable one from another.

From time to time //Kushay commented to Tsamgao with apparent reference to some trees or clump of bushes and this seemed to decide which clearing we entered next. Finally she plunged into a candle-pod thicket like any other we had passed and pointed to a three square metre patch of low plants with tiny purple flowers which shed their petals when we tried to pick them. It was the root of this plant that was used, she said.

How had she known where to find it, we asked. Tsamgao questioned her. 'She found them here last year,' he said.

This incident illustrated for us how Bushmen accumulate the considerable knowledge of plants that enables them to spread their risk over a wide range of different species that are not all likely to fail at the same time. They do not simply wander about hopefully in search of food. They know where the productive areas are, where particular plants grow, when they ripen and in what quantities they are likely to be found, and they plan their lives accordingly. Yet they do not ruthlessly exploit their environment but use it wisely, never taking from it more of anything than they need, always leaving a little behind so that there will be a new crop the following year. By careful observation over generations they have gained an intimate understanding of the habits of their plants. Everything is noted, discussed and shared, and thus they have survived, where men with a more aggressive approach to nature and a more competitive attitude towards one another would have foundered.

Tsamgao, like other Bushmen, knows about plants, where they may be found and what they may be used for. He even knows that they breathe and drink and that in some way they eat. He knows the way things are but not why they are so. It strikes him as an impertinence to question why the Creator made plants and animals to act as they do.

'Those are things the old people never told us about,' he says.

THE HEART OF THE HUNTER

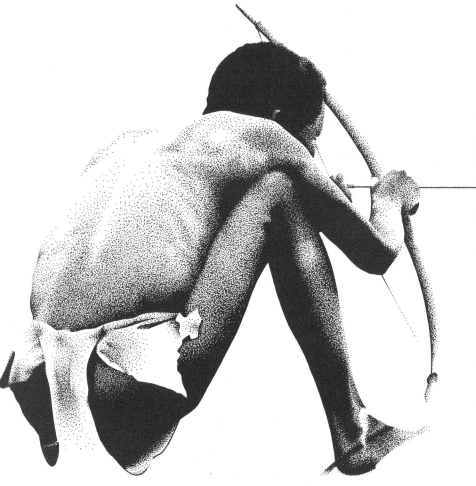

The !Kung Bushmen say that their short autumn, which comes in April, is the best of all the seasons. Apart from a rare vagrant shower, the heavy rains are past, but there is still water in small pans scattered about their territories. The Big Rains have driven away the great heat of spring and early summer. The biting cold that lengthens winter's nights has not yet set in. Men range farther. There is ripe plant food everywhere, and the larger antelope, having calved a month or two ago, are now sleek and fat and much more plentiful. This above all is the season of the hunter.

Meat may be only a small part of their diet, a flavouring in leaner times for their staple vegetable, but it is the food they most desire. Their esteem for meat is so high that the Bushmen place the hunter at the centre of the system of practices and observances that regulate their little societies, in which all men are hunters. For a man is by definition a hunter. A male who does not hunt remains a child and may not marry, for how can he expect to take a wife if he cannot bring meat home for his family and parents-in-law and skins in which to clothe his wife and children?

In a young man's life, no event is more significant than when he shoots his first large antelope, for then he becomes a man among men, and his father performs the Rite of the First Kill that marks the youth's passage from adolescence to manhood, rubbing a ritually purified compound of charred meat and fat into shallow incisions in his son's skin. In some bands the rites are performed twice, the incisions being made down the right side for the first male animal killed, and down his left side when he shoots his first female animal. These 'tattoos' are potent magic to ensure that at the very core of his being he will be an intrepid and indefatigable hunter; that there will be an inner force compelling him to hunt – that he will have the 'heart of the hunter'.

The !Kung use the same word to describe the marking of the young hunter as for the branding of the animals when, in the story told by the old people, the kori bustard fanned the flames of the eternal fire with his great wings to heat the irons used by ≠Gao!na to brand first the zebra with his stripes, and then the eland, hartebeest, ostrich, gemsbok, duiker and all the other animals with their markings, ending with the black-backed jackal and the brown hyaena.

It is intriguing to speculate on the inner significance of this ritual identification of man and animal, of the hunter with his quarry, just as it is fascinating to consider the possibility that a key insight into the Bushman cosmos is afforded by their reversal of the usual order in

their belief that all the animals were once people. Does this mean that they experience
themselves and the creatures about them in a way that is fundamentally different to that of other men, whose science tells them that people were once animals, and whose religions place man at the pinnacle of creation?

Certainly, the light weapons used by the Bushmen do not give them any great advantage over the animals, and for the hunter to succeed there must be a close mental identification with his quarry.

According to the /Gwi Bushmen today, N!odima, the creator, is the giver of life. All animals belong to him and their lives may not be taken lightly. A man may kill for food and in self-defence, but wanton killing will be punished, and care should be taken to avoid accidental killing, even to the extent of preventing a scorpion from running into the fire. They see themselves as protectors of the animals. When they kill for food they try to minimise the animal's suffering by moving in as quickly as possible after the poison begins to take effect to deliver the *coup de grâce* with their spears.

Anthropologists who have spent long periods with !Kung bands say that they seem to be less sensitive to the pain and suffering of the animals they kill. They hunt and kill dispassionately, saying simply that it is in the nature of hunters to kill animals. Nevertheless, they show respect for the lives they take, never killing more than they can eat, and not wasting any part of an animal that falls to their arrows.

An experience which illustrates how dangerous it is to generalise about Bushman attitudes, even when dealing with members of the same language group who live not far from one another, has to do with a small superstition of mine concerning the praying mantis.

As a result of reading old texts on the mythology of the Cape Bushmen, in which Mantis is a prominent figure, I began regarding it as a sign of good luck if a mantis alighted on me at the start of a visit to the Bushmen. And somehow, whenever we set out, a mantis appeared and our trip was successful.

On our trip to Tsumkwe, however, no mantis appeared during the first few days and I began feeling irrationally uneasy. And then, while we were eating lunch around our campfire one midday, a mantis landed on my sleeve. I stood up carefully and walked a short distance away, not wanting the mantis to fly from me into the fire.

I knew from my reading that the mantis does not feature in the folklore of the present-day !Kung, but more than one writer suggests that they have a special attitude towards the mantis; that they fear it as a 'death thing', because it enjoys the special protection of ≠Goa!na, who will punish them if they allow harm to befall one.

I was shocked that evening, therefore, when, as we sat around the fire with a crowd of !Kung children, a gentle boy named Kangori picked up a mantis that had landed within the circle of light and casually tossed it into the flames.

Long ago, the Bushmen who roamed the hunting grounds of the Cape and the tiny mountain kingdom of Lesotho, believed that their Mantis hero, the first being, was creator of the antelope and the protector of his creation. They also believed that respect for the animals was essential if they were to be successful in the hunt; that they would not be able to kill if there were no respect. Thus there was a definite psychic link between the hunter and his prey. This connection was recognised in the observance which precluded hunters from eating or even handling springbok meat, for fear that this would give their quarry the fleetness of the springbok and that, even if they succeeded in lodging a poisoned arrow in its flesh, it would remain awake and active during the night and escape from them while they slept.

Although the creation myths of Bushmen living in different parts of the country are as varied as the languages and dialects they speak, and probably for the same reason, one thing they all have in common is the belief that there was once a time when all the animals were people. The scene changes, the characters differ and the plot is altered, but the theme remains the same.

The Bushmen who lived along the middle course of the Orange River more than 100 years ago attributed the diversity of animals and the distinction between them and people to the behaviour of a quarrelsome mythical individual who fought with every animal of the 'early race' and tried to injure it. Eventually he disappeared without trace, but his last vengeful act was to change all the animals into their present form.

Bushmen living at the time lower down the Orange believed that people and all animals had originated together in a hole in the ground, from which they came speaking the same language. Throughout a full day they issued in a continuous stream from this hole between the roots of a giant tree that spread its branches over a vast territory. When the sun set they all gathered beneath the tree for the night. The Creator warned the people that, no matter how cold it became during the night, they were not to light a fire. But it grew steadily colder, until just before dawn, when the people could no longer endure the cold, they lit one. Immediately the animals took fright at the blaze and stampeded, losing their powers of speech in their panic. And ever since that time they have fled from man.

The tradition in which the Bushmen who formerly occupied the slopes of the faraway Maluti Mountains in Lesotho accounted for the separation between people and animals also features their Mantis hero, /Kaggen, the first being, who made all things by ordering them to appear. Thus he created the sun, moon, stars, wind, mountains and animals. The story of how the latter came into being and were 'spoilt' begins with a quarrel between /Kaggen and his wife over a knife she made blunt by using it to sharpen her digging stick. As a result of his anger, she gives birth to an eland calf in the fields.

/Kaggen leaves the calf in the bush while he goes away for three days to obtain arrow poison. But while he is away, his two sons find the calf while out hunting and, not knowing what it is, they kill it for food. On his return /Kaggen is angry and accuses his sons of 'spoiling' the elands before he had perfected them. He instructs his sons to put the blood of the calf in a pot and churn it with a stick.

At the first attempt, the blood splatters and becomes snakes. They try again and the blood that is spilt turns into hartebeest that run away.

/Kaggen is still not satisfied. He orders his wife to clean out the pot and to bring fresh blood from the paunch of the little eland. To this he adds fat from the heart, and when the blood spatters this time, each drop becomes an eland bull, and all the bulls surround /Kaggen and his sons and menace them with their horns. 'See how you have spoilt the elands,' says /Kaggen, and he chases them away.

The next time the blood is churned it produces eland cows, in such numbers that the earth is covered with them. 'Now go and hunt them and try to kill one,' says /Kaggen. 'That is now your work, for it was you who spoilt them.' But they fail, and so /Kaggen himself goes out and spears three bulls. Thereafter, with his blessing, his sons are also successful.

The Maluti Bushmen used to say that on that day people were given the game animals to eat, and that it was in this way that the animals were 'spoilt' and became wild.

When in the early 1870s J. M. Orpen recorded this tradition while on a magisterial tour of the district, he asked his informants where /Kaggen was to be found. 'We do not know, but the eland do,' they replied. 'Have you not hunted and heard his cry, when the eland suddenly start and run to his call? Where he is, eland are in droves like cattle.'

It is easy to imagine how, before other men came and found new uses for the more verdant regions of southern Africa, the hillsides and plains must have been spread with great herds of antelope; particularly eland, whose ox-like bulk, appearance and docility led naturally to their being described as the indigenous 'cattle' of Africa.

Antelope are the most popular subject in many rock art sites in the subcontinent, and the eland is the most frequently painted of all the animals. It is the eland too that is painted to the highest perfection, even in the remote Tsodilo Hills, and some latter-day interpreters have suggested on these grounds that there may once have been an eland cult among the Bushmen.

Whether or not this was so, the eland still has an especially favoured place in the Bushman hierarchy of animal food preferences, for eland continue to range over large areas of the Kalahari in herds of up to a few hundred, browsing in the thickets and obtaining water from the grass, leaves and melons they eat. In terms of the energy expended compared with the size of the reward, hunting the relatively placid eland renders an excellent return, for a full-grown bull may weigh more than a metric ton. They are particularly prized for their fat, of which they yield considerably more than other antelope. The Bushmen use it to soften their skins and to preserve the wooden handles of their weapons and implements, and they mix it with powdered red stone for painting designs on the faces of brides during marriage rites. What is more the most ancient of all !Kung music is the 'eland music' that is sung only by women and only when they dance the 'eland dance' in celebration of a young girl's first menstruation.

Although the climate of the Kalahari may seem forbidding, these thirstlands support a large number of animals of many kinds that are well adapted to austerity. Some are physically equipped to obtain all the moisture they need from their food. Many know the bulbs and roots that store water and dig for them with their hooves. A few can sense when it rains a great distance away and move swiftly to take advantage of it. Yet others migrate in the dry season to permanent watering-places on the fringes of the Kalahari, and only return when it rains.

But the great animal migrations of a century and more ago are now something of the past. Many of the permanent waterholes on the edges of the Kalahari have been absorbed into human settlement and have been fenced off to prevent the spread of stock diseases, with the result that animals such as elephant, buffalo, zebra and impala can no longer move freely with the seasons. Cut off from these vital supplementary water sources, the wildebeest, or gnu, no longer roam over the wide grassy plains and open woodlands in such vast herds as they did formerly. In particularly dry years they die in great numbers.

The dense undergrowth in the thickets provides food and shelter for insects and the spiders, scorpions, lizards and birds that feed on them. The leafy trees and shrubs lure herbivores large and small, from tiny rodents and lesser antelope, such as the solitary steenbok and duiker and the gregarious springbok, to the gemsbok, hartebeest and giraffe. Birds of prey, insectivores and small flesh-eaters, including the jackal, bat-eared fox, aardwolf, caracal, genet and wildcat, come to prey here on the insects, mice, ground squirrels, birds, hares and snakes, while the larger antelope attract lion, leopard, cheetah and wild dog. The hyaenas wait on the sidelines and high in the sky vultures circle over a kill.

Bushmen fit into this ecosystem at more than one level; they compete with all the animals for water, snare the prey of the smaller carnivores, rival the lions and other big predators for the larger game and contest the claims of the scavengers to fresh carrion.

But Bushman hunting is not sufficiently intensive to disturb the natural balance. They have hunted in the same way for a considerable period in their present areas without depleting them of game. Because they are so few and because their sustenance comes from so many different points in the food-web, no single animal species is endangered by them. They kill only to consume, and their usual method of hunting is so gentle that they create less disturbance than a lion or leopard making its kill and do not frighten the animals away from the hunting grounds.

The silent flight of an arrow is followed by a moment of shock when the metal point bites into the soft flesh of its victim. The wounded animal's mute panic sends the rest of the herd scampering off to a short distance, from which they gaze back apprehensively with ears cocked at the scene of recent trauma. Then one by one they lower their heads once again and resume their leisurely browsing, while the wounded animal falls behind and is dispatched and butchered out of sight of its fellows.

When Bushmen still inhabited the more hospitable parts of the subcontinent, they often trapped the hippopotamus and other large animals by digging deep holes large enough to accommodate the animal in busy game paths, armed them with pointed stakes coated with poison and set upright at the bottom, and covered them over lightly with thin branches and leaves. Early travellers and explorers complained frequently in their journals that in the vicinity of rivers they walked in constant danger of a fatal accident, because there were so many of these pitfalls so cunningly concealed. But in the Kalahari there are no busy game paths used regularly by animals on their way to water, and so pitfalls are not dug by the Bushmen who live there.

A method of hunting elephant, used in olden times, was to steal up behind one of them and then dart in and hamstring it with a single swift axe blow, incapacitating it so that it might be speared to death with impunity.

After lions make a kill, the Bushmen know when the beasts have satisfied their hunger but not yet eaten enough to make them sluggish, and they select this moment to drive the big cats off and take what is left of the meat for themselves.

Very young antelope are sometimes run to earth on foot or brought down with throwing clubs; birds and small mammals are caught in ingenious snares; the porcupine, antbear and warthog are flushed from their burrows with smoke or dug out from above and speared; and the big leopard tortoise needs only to be rolled on to its back and baked in its shell. But bow and arrow are still the chief weapon of the hunt.

It is not possible to tell from existing evidence when it was that the Bushmen first discovered the use of poison and began hunting by this method, but specimens of arrowheads found in several Stone Age sites in southern Africa confirm that the four-part composite arrow made to carry poison by the Bushmen today was in long-established use at least 5 000 years ago.

Before iron became available to them in comparatively recent times through trade with other people, Bushmen tipped their arrows with tiny flakes of quartz set in vegetable mastic, and carved arrowheads from bone and ivory, sometimes with chips of stone and the points of porcupine quills gummed to the shanks and barbs. Today the /Gwi Bushmen in the central Kalahari still sometimes carve bone arrowheads from the core of gemsbok horns, splitting it into flat strips and shaping it before it dries out and becomes hard and brittle, but the universal material from which arrowheads are now made is heavy gauge fencing wire, cut into lengths of about ten centimetres.

The gracile conception and design of the Bushman arrow is singularly consistent with the essential character and genius of the people responsible for its perfection, for it is not a crude instrument of brute force but a silent harbinger of death; the wasp-sting of little people in a vast landscape. It carries no more weight and is propelled by no greater force than necessary; the hunter relies on subtler ways of achieving his purpose, which is not to kill outright with the extent of the wound it inflicts, but to inject potent slow-acting poison into the bloodstream of the victim.

Its composite construction is a practical design feature. It takes a man a little more than two days to make the components and assemble such an arrow, although he would not go to all the trouble to make only one arrow at a time.

Old Tame is well-known in the Tsumkwe area for his true arrows. Many men carry in

their quivers one or more made by him. This pleases old Tame, because if any of the hunters
is successful with one of his arrows, he benefits in the distribution of the meat.

The first time we visited him we found him sitting outside his hut in the shade of a light platform, supported by four stout poles, on which cooking and other utensils were stacked to keep them off the ground. He was flattening one end of a ten to 12 centimetre length of heavy wire with deftly placed hammer blows, using a short section of steel rail for an anvil. Several similar pieces of straight wire lay on an irregular piece of hide in front of him.

Old Tame delivered a few last taps with his hammer, held the piece of wire up to the light and nodded his approval. Then he started giving the flattened end the typical broadhead shape with a file.

He said that he learnt his craft from his father, who, he admitted, was a better fletcher than he, because his father did not have the advantages of steel hammer, anvil and file, but used pieces of stone for all three purposes. He worked as he spoke, his fingers nimble and sensitive, though calloused, the whorls on the pads inlaid with grime.

When next we saw him two days later he had a row of sparkling new arrow points, each shaped to delicate perfection, leaning against a stick of firewood beside him. Now he was using his file to fashion selected fragments of bone into small spindle-shaped pieces about six centimetres long and slightly less than a centimetre in diameter in the middle, tapering to a point at both ends.

We had to wait a few more days before Tsamgao took us to watch old Tame assembling an arrow from the components he had made. For the main shaft, the old man took a smooth 35 centimetre length of thin reed from between two joints, cut away the harder material of the joint at one end and notched it at the other to take a bowstring. He then fitted the unshaped end of the iron point into one end of a short reed collar and glued it in position with acacia gum. The main shaft and forepart of the arrow were then united by the bone linkshaft, one point of which was gummed into the back of the reed collar.

Old Tame inserted the other point of the linkshaft into the leading end of the main shaft but did not fix it with gum. This joint is never gummed, he explained, because the shaft is meant to part from the poisoned foresection at this point if the wounded animal attempts to pluck the arrow out with its teeth or tries to dislodge it by rubbing up against a tree.

Finally, he reinforced the reed collar and both ends of the main shaft with fine bindings of gummed sinews to prevent splitting on impact and to protect the nock against splintering under pressure from the bowstring. He bound the full length of the iron shank in the same way, from behind the broadhead point to the reed collar, to give it a better adhesive surface for the poison.

'This is a good arrow,' said Tsamgao when it was finished. 'I am a Bushman. I know a good arrow.'

The Bushman bow that shoots these unflighted projectiles is appropriately light and is usually made from a green brandybush branch or sapling about a metre long and two to three centimetres thick in the middle, tapering equally towards both ends and strengthened with suitably placed bindings of neck sinew. With a pull of less than ten kilograms, it is capable of sending such an arrow 100 metres, but the effective range is only a quarter of that. This limitation has had a profound effect on the development of the Bushman's hunting skills and, indeed, on his whole way of life.

In all save exceptional instances such light weaponry would be hopelessly inadequate without poison for either hunting or war. But Bushmen were expert toxicologists thousands of years before other peoples appeared in their hunting grounds. The poisons they used varied from one locality to another and according to the purposes for which they were used. In the eastern parts of the Cape they made a powerful brew of snake venom, euphorbia milk and the juice of the succulent *Amaryllis disticha*. The Bushmen living along the upper

Orange, Vaal and Caledon rivers concocted a similar mixture and laced it for good measure with crushed scorpions and trap-door spiders. Where pools were stocked they used the milk of the euphorbia as a fish poison.

But of all the Bushman poisons the most awesome for its virulence was and still is prepared from the grubs of the *Diamphidia* and *Polyclada* beetles that feed on the leaves of the *Commiphora africana* and certain marula trees.

Where colonies of the beetles are found, the cocoons containing the grubs are dug from the ground under these trees and stored in a horn container for future use. Today, this is the only poison used by Bushmen in the central Kalahari, and, although the !Kung in the north-west have a lesser vegetable poison as an alternative, it is only resorted to when supplies of *Diamphidia* and *Polyclada* run out.

Tsamgao's son ≠Toma brought us a message from his father one morning that old Tame had obtained a fresh supply of poison and would be dressing his new arrows with it that day. We hurried to his camp.

The old man had set out his arrows across two parallel sticks to keep them out of the sand. As we arrived he opened his horn container and tipped several *Diamphidia* cocoons on to his patch of hide. Then, one by one, he opened the cocoons carefully and shook out the grubs, each of which he rolled gently back and forth in the palm of his hand to soften its insides without breaking its skin.

He handled the grubs expertly but with obvious caution. Then taking one between thumb and forefinger he plucked one of its front legs from its socket. Squeezing the grub like a miniature tube of toothpaste, he dabbed the reddish liquid that issued from it along the full length of the sinew-bound metal shank of an arrow. Each arrow required the liquid from several grubs, and the process was repeated many times before all of old Tame's arrows had received their first coating of poison and lay drying in the sun.

Meanwhile Tame mixed more of the liquid with a sticky vegetable extract on a flat piece of stone, and when the first coat was dry he applied a second, thicker coat with a twig.

When this poison is injected into the bloodstream by an arrow, it causes convulsions, paralysis and death. In the case of smaller antelope, death may come within 24 hours, while larger animals may take two or three days to succumb. But once it is in the blood, its action can be neither checked nor reversed. There is no known antidote that can save animal or man.

The hunter-adventurer, James Chapman, who in the middle of the last century travelled through the central Kalahari on his way to the Victoria Falls, claimed that the Bushmen revealed to him that the antidote was a species of root that was much favoured by the steenbok and duiker and grew in the very soil in which the poison grubs were found. It is interesting to note that the /Gwi living in the same area today, although they admit to knowledge of no certain antidote, say that the effects of a very small dose of the poison may be reduced by chewing the bulb of the *Ammocaris coranica* and massaging its juice into the wound.

Cases of fatal accidents with poison and instances when unbridled anger ended with an arrow are sufficiently common for all Bushmen to have a very clear understanding of the consequences. Poison is one of the supports on which their lives depend, but it is also a caution and a threat. They need it and use it, but they also fear it. Their respect for it has shaped their way of life.

The missionary John Campbell left a vivid record of the effects of arrow poison on humans in the journal of his travels over a century and a half ago, and the account he gave of the suffering of a companion wounded in the shoulder by a Bushman, makes chilling reading still.

'We did everything for the poor wounded man in our power by cutting out the flesh all

round the wound, administering *eau de luce*, and laudanum to mitigate the pain; but he lay
groaning the whole night,' Campbell wrote. 'At half past one, his pain was so great that we were obliged to halt . . . to lay him down under a bush from which he was never to rise. His appearance alarmed us, being greatly swelled, particularly about the head and throat. He said that he felt the poison gradually work downwards to his very toes, and then ascend in the same manner; as it ascended his body swelled . . . He thought he felt the chief strength of the poison to lodge in one of his cheeks, and requested that the cheek might be cut off, which we did not comply with, persuaded that his whole frame was equally contaminated. The Bushman we had with us said in the morning that he would die immediately on the going down of the sun, which he certainly did; for the sun had not dipped beneath the horizon five minutes before he breathed his last. His countenance was frightful, being so disfigured by the swelling. On his brow was a swelling as large as a goose egg.'

With such fearsome reputation, it is not surprising that poison assumes greater significance than a mere hunting aid for the Bushmen. In their little traditional societies it is the ultimate sanction which makes their state of benign anarchy possible, enabling them to live together without regulation by authority and yet manage to avoid internal violence.

Within Bushman bands to this day, everything possible is done to defuse situations that could lead to clashes between individuals in which poisoned arrows might eventually be exchanged. If it reaches this stage, both belligerents are likely to die in lingering agony. No dispute that is pushed to the ultimate is likely to be won by either of them. Short of this, they must back down, rise above their differences or negotiate reconciliation.

In their relations with other bands and their early contacts with strange peoples, the poisoned arrow was the Stone Age equivalent of a nuclear deterrent. The Bushman was not warlike without provocation, but he had a name for defending what he regarded as his own with the desperate courage that often comes with the realisation that, if you are to survive, there is no alternative to war. Nevertheless, he did not make war lightly, because his weapons were capable of delivering certain death, painful death, but not instant death. The slow action of the poison left a stricken adversary ample time in which to avenge the suffering that lay ahead of him.

Other peoples, mindful of the Bushmen's reputation as fearless fighters and the deadly certainty of their poison, considered it more prudent to leave them alone if there was no direct clash of interests. But clashes between huntsman and pastoralist were inevitable and grew more frequent, and attitudes hardened on both sides. The first firearms the Bushmen faced were effective over roughly the same distance as their bows; to get safely within range of them their opponents were obliged to advance behind moveable oxhide screens. But it was a war waged sporadically over more than 200 years, and their poison lost its deterrent effect when finally they faced guns that could dispose of them from beyond the range of their bows. Then they fought to the last man, and he fought to his last arrow.

Many died less heroic deaths, smoked from their caves of refuge, slaughtered about their fires, but records of encounters written by their adversaries, often reveal acts of great bravery by the Bushmen; of men who, after releasing their last arrow, hurled themselves off precipices or met the bullets with their faces covered to hide their death agony from their foe. The dust of countless forgotten heroes is mingled now with the earth the Bushmen once thought was theirs alone.

But armed resistance did not save the Bushmen then, as it cannot preserve them now from the insidious pressures that are subverting their old way of life. Today the bow and poisoned arrow serve only their primary purpose as weapons of the hunt.

Hunting is the great masculine activity among the Bushmen. Men hunt from adolescence until they grow too old. When they are not actually hunting they are talking about their hunting experiences or repairing their weapons. Man is the hunter. Women may snare birds and pick up snakes and insects for food, but only men may hunt. For a woman to so much as touch a man's bow and arrows could impair his skill, deprive him of luck and weaken his hunter's heart.

The territory in which a Bushman band may hunt does not necessarily correspond exactly to their gathering territory and often spills over into the gathering territories of their neighbours. This is because of what the Bushmen see as the basic difference between plants and animals: plants are rooted in one place and so naturally seem to belong to the 'owners' of the place, but animals wander about from one band's domain to another. Thus hunting rights seem to be less strictly territorial. Some Bushmen say that animals belong to whomever shoots them, and a band finding the spoor of an animal in their own preserve will track it down and shoot it even if it has moved into a neighbouring territory. But they will generally give some of the meat to the people of the place, as territorial rights are not ignored completely. The flexibility of this system has reciprocal benefits, for every band experiences times when neighbouring territories abound with game, while their territory has none. But territory is a more important determinant with some bands than with others, and where greater concentrations of people sharpen the competition for food, the territorial principle may be strictly enforced.

Bushmen eat a wide range of mammals, birds, reptiles and insects, but the flesh of some animals is taboo to certain people according to their age, sex and whether or not they are married and have children. These taboos, we found, vary from one band to another. Thus, when we asked a Bushman whether it was permissible to eat a particular animal, his reply was usually framed with qualifications such as: 'Yes, it is eaten, but I may not eat it because I have only two children,' or 'We living here may not eat it, but other people do.'

Most taboos, it appears, apply to animals that are too small to be shared by many people. By limiting the categories of people who are permitted to eat them, more opportunities are created for the very young and the aged to eat meat. Ostrich eggs, for example, may only be eaten in some bands by women, children and old men, but not by men of hunting age. The flesh of steenbok and springhare may be forbidden to married adults with babies less than a year old, while the tortoise and kori bustard may be food only for elderly people and infants. Often only old women eat snakes, while the meat of large male antelope is taboo to girls and young women. There is a general aversion to the meat of the larger predators and scavengers, mainly because they are man-eaters, but among some Bushmen living in the central Kalahari, there are times when the extremes of hunger permit old people to eat the flesh of lions, and in times of exceptional austerity even the hyaena is eaten.

The animals most frequently killed for food are the smaller species, but they are generally snared or, like the springhare, caught by other means. They are not deliberately hunted. A man will shoot one if he comes upon it by chance in circumstances which favour success, but the larger antelope are the real marks he seeks for his arrows. But these are also the animals which are most difficult to hunt. They are often scarce and are not easy to stalk undetected.

We noted that men often go out to hunt day after day without success. They leave early in the morning and return just before nightfall, weary and feeling the pangs of hunger and thirst, having covered anything from ten to 30 kilometres in the heat of the day. But they are off again next morning, impelled by their hunter's hearts to persist until they find a fresh trail of an animal that is worth tracking.

The hunter does not encumber himself with anything more than he needs to carry. He does not even take food and water with him for the day, as these will hinder him and limit his ability to move about swiftly. His hunting equipment is light and functional, and he carries it all over one shoulder.

He keeps his arrows in a quiver made from a tube of root bark capped with a gemsbok scrotum. In some parts of the country occupied by Bushmen in former times, the quiver was made of leather, and in the region of the lower Orange River it was made from the bark of the tree aloe commonly called the kokerboom, or quiver tree. But the root bark of either the camelthorn or the false umbrella thorn is the usual material today.

Quivers we examined generally contained five or more arrows, the hunter's fire-making sticks, a sharpened stick for holding meat over the flames, a hollow sip-stick for sucking up any moisture that may have collected in the hollows of trees or a little below the surface of the sand, and a stick with blobs of gum and vegetable mastic for making running repairs to his equipment while in the field. He carries his bow slung between slits at either end of the shoulder strap where it is attached to the quiver, and his short spear is carried in the same position, with the point held fast between the bark and leather binding at the base. His digging stick, knife and other small items he may need on the hunt are carried in a shoulder bag made from the whole skin of a steenbok, duiker or warthog.

We never saw men going out singly to hunt. This, we were told, is because, if successful, they will not be able to carry all the meat home alone and some of it will go to waste. Usually, the size of a hunting party depends on the time they intend remaining away and the kind of animal they are hunting. If they intend remaining away overnight the party may be fairly large, and as many as a dozen may include themselves in a giraffe hunt, but they normally hunt in pairs or groups of three or four.

Hunting is not a competitive activity, since effectively they are all hunting for the benefit of the whole band, and thus there may be much discussion but little dispute about where they will hunt. Guided by the divining tablets, which are thrown at the outset, small parties grouped around hunters of repute go off in different directions from their camp to search for game, so giving themselves a greater chance of communal success than if they all were to go together in one direction.

As animals are alert and the range of their weapons is short, the Bushmen need to have a very good understanding of animal behaviour. Man does not possess the highly developed sense of smell that guides other large predators to their prey, and so his success as a predator depends almost entirely on the accuracy of his observations and his ability to interpret the almost imperceptible clues to an animal's movements which it leaves behind it in the sand and on the grass and bushes. Once the Bushmen start tracking their quarry, all their knowledge of animals is brought to bear on the interpretation of the spoor.

Whenever we accompanied a hunting party into the veld the Bushmen had no objection to our remaining close to them during the early stages, while they were still looking for a fresh spoor or while the animal they were tracking was still reckoned to be far off, but as soon as they felt we were coming within smell, sound or sight of it, we were expected to hang back and avoid betraying their presence to their quarry.

'You are big people. The ground moves when you walk,' we were told tactfully.

Usually, we seemed to wander about a good deal at the start of a hunt, while the Bushmen inspected likely places for signs of animals. Sometimes this went on all day without their discovering any worthwhile prospects. At other times they found a fresh spoor fairly quickly, and then the hunt began in earnest.

The hunters examine the trail minutely. Everything is noticed, considered and discussed. The kink in a trodden grass blade, the direction of the pull that broke a twig from a bush, the depth, size, shape and disposition of the tracks themselves, all reveal information about the condition of the animal or herd, which direction it is moving in, the rate of travel and what its future movements are likely to be.

There is continuous subdued chatter among the hunters as they develop from their observations theories about what the animals are doing, or modify earlier theories in the light of fresh clues provided by the trail.

For our part, we had to observe the Bushmen, very much as they observe the animals, to infer from their actions what was going on. It was not possible for us to have an interpreter translate what they were saying while the hunt was in progress, but as they remember a hunt in detail and love to recall it afterwards, it was fairly easy for us to find out from them after the hunt why they had acted as they did at different stages.

When the Bushmen come close enough to see the animals they are tracking or locate them precisely, the hunt enters its crucial phases. All talk ceases and the hunters communicate with hand signals. If the bush offers good cover, they pause in concealment to watch the herd and ascertain from its grazing pattern whether it is likely to remain in the same place for a while or is about to move on, whether the animals are nervous or unaware of the hunters' approach.

In selecting which animal in the herd will be their victim, the Bushmen's main consideration is its size and, therefore, the quantity of meat it will provide for them. But the importance of size may be outweighed by other considerations. If the animal they select runs a long distance before lying down to die, they will have to pursue it farther and carry its meat back over a longer distance. From long experience they are able to tell which of the animals is more likely to remain in the vicinity after being struck by an arrow.

The season, time of day, temperature, wind direction, terrain and the positions of the other animals are all taken into account in working out a stalking strategy.

But the Bushmen do not delay in taking these decisions. They know that the longer they wait the more chance they give their prey of detecting their presence, and particularly where there is little cover for them, their aim is to move to within bowshot as quickly as possible.

On one occasion the hunting party we were with tracked down a gemsbok over the better part of the day and at last they had it virtually within their grasp. Three of them snaked through the grass to almost within range, and then a fourth, who had remained further back, coughed. It was only a small cough, but it was enough. The gemsbok swung its head towards them with its rapier sharp horns lowered. But in the same instant it seemed to change its mind and, wheeling suddenly, it raced off. The three hunters immediately sprang to their feet and ran after it, vainly firing their arrows at its departing hooves.

Although they had wasted a day under trying conditions, the Bushmen accepted their loss in a good spirit, and even seemed to see a funny side to the incident. They spoke about it for days afterwards.

But there were successful hunts too.

One day our hunting party tracked down a small herd of kudu in some bushy country. The Bushmen watched them in absolute silence and, having selected their victim and decided on their strategy, put down their bags and other equipment and began stalking it, carrying only their bows and arrows.

They advanced as rapidly as they could in a stooping posture that made them look like other animals to the weak-sighted kudu. Wind direction and other conditions favoured the hunters, but there was always the chance that a fly would carry their scent to inform the herd that the blurred figures were actually men. When the animals turned away from their browse, the hunters froze; when they resumed eating, the men moved closer.

As they drew nearer the hunters dropped to their elbows and knees and crawled forward, with their arrows already fitted to their bowstrings, and the moment they came within range they let fly a stream of arrows at their victim.

The first twang of the bowstrings alerted the kudu and it spun round, but already it was too late, for two poisoned arrows were embedded in its flesh, one in the shoulder and one in the rump. It uttered a hoarse bark, and the whole herd lumbered off, throwing up their tails and revealing the white undersides.

The Bushmen did not go after them. They went to the spot where the victim had been
standing and examined its tracks, memorising individual characteristics, so that they would be able to tell its spoor from the tracks left by the rest of the herd.

It was not necessary to give chase immediately, the Bushmen told us. The wounded animal would soon fall behind the rest and, as it was already late afternoon, it would not run far before nightfall. During the night it would remain nearby. As there were no recent signs of predators in the vicinity, it could safely be left until morning, by which time it would be considerably weakened by the effects of two securely placed arrows.

Next morning, accompanied by other men who came to help carry home the meat, the hunters quickly picked up the spoor of the wounded kudu. Now its trail had new features to be evaluated by the Bushmen. Its dung was examined for any indication it might give of the condition of the animal. Traces of blood on fallen leaves and smears on grass and bushes along the trail provided information about the severity of the wounds.

By midday it was obvious that the kudu could not be far off. Bloodstains on the ground showed where it had paused to rest at shorter and shorter intervals. Larger patches of blood told the story of how, as it weakened, it had lain down and then struggled to get up again.

Eventually we came to where the kudu had lain down for the last time. For a while it attempted to keep the hunters at bay with its horns, but then it became too weary for even this defence, and the hunters darted in and speared it through the heart.

After making a kill the Bushmen usually butcher the animal on the spot and, depending on the distance from their camp, the meat is either carried home in large pieces or, if there is some danger of the meat going off on the long homeward haul, it is cut into thin strips and hung on bushes, where the hot dry air quickly covers them with a protective airtight film that allows them to dry out towards the centre without rotting.

The spoils of the hunt are shared, but the meat of small animals is allocated only to the members of the hunting party and through them to their immediate families, while the meat of large animals is divided between all members of the band. The traditional patterns of distribution varies from place to place, but the effect is the same: they all eat.

The system of sharing among the !Kung, which is more elaborate than the system of other Bushmen, seems to have been evolved for the purpose of eliminating any notion that the meat belongs to the man who actually shot the animal.

After making a kill, all members of the hunting party have a right to remove, cook and eat the liver and other portions of the carcass that are likely to decay soonest. Thereafter, rights to the meat are vested not in the hand that released the fatal arrow but in the arrow itself. The men are continually making presents of arrows to one another or lending them to those who are going hunting when they are not. It is customary that the man to whom the arrow currently belongs is the nominal 'owner' of the flesh it brings down. Initially, he distributes the meat between himself, the man who originally made the arrow and the members of the hunting party. Each of them then gives the best of his own portion to his parents-in-law and discharges his responsibilities to his wife, children and parents. Finally, he gives to his more distant relatives and friends from whom he has received meat in the past. The system even encourages generosity, for the more liberal you are towards others, the more open-handed they will feel obliged to be towards you.

Sharing serves the obvious practical purpose of making sure that all the meat is eaten while it is still relatively fresh, but it is also a vital unifying force in Bushman society, and no man would dream of acquiring meat and not sharing it, even if he could do so without being found out. On the social level, sharing safeguards the survival of the whole band and not only its more successful members. Some do not become fat while others are reduced to skin and bone by a period of continuous failure. There is no cause for jealousy, which could tear their societies apart, and the constantly changing but ever-present network of reciprocal obligations maintained by institutionalised sharing holds the members of the band together.

A hunting skill that also has an important social application as a deterrent to deviant behaviour is the finely developed aptitude that Bushmen have for translating what they see in animal tracks into a detailed account of what the animals have been doing. As Bushmen themselves say, the sand reveals everything. Members of a band know the footprints of all their fellows, and there is scant chance of an adultery going undetected or a thief not being identified by people who are able to describe the mating ceremonies of nocturnal animals, although they have never witnessed them, but have read it all in the sand. What is written by footprints is as vivid for them as if it had been enacted before their eyes.

Bushmen acquire an extensive knowledge of animal behaviour through constant observation, careful attention to detail and continual discussion among themselves of what they have seen. Their understanding enables them to identify completely with the animal they are hunting, so that they can answer questions such as: 'What would I do now if I were this animal?' And their replies are amazingly accurate. Such anthropomorphic projection is rejected by scientists, who say it is not possible to equate human and animal consciousness, but perhaps it comes more easily to men who believe that all the animals were once people like themselves.

THE ETERNAL FIRE

It is winter from May to August in the regions inhabited by the Bushmen. The equatorial airs that moved southward in summer have once again receded, and the warmth that lingered into autumn gives way quite suddenly to the coldest of the seasons. The Kalahari, more than 1 000 metres above sea-level and beyond the reach of the Indian Ocean's warming touch at this time of year, feels instead the keen edge of temperatures that plunge at night to below freezing, and even the days may be painfully cold when the south wind slices through the interior, beneath cloudless azure skies from which not a drop of rain falls.

For the Bushmen, the cold is less bearable than the heat. Among those who must live beside their waterholes at this time, there are more people in camp than at any other, huddling in their gemsbok hide cloaks about the fires with their backs turned to the wind, for no one goes out to hunt or gather when the south wind blows. This is when fire, always a centre of social and spiritual life, acquires its greatest immediate significance.

It is interesting that fire features in more than one Bushman tradition concerning the differentiation between animals and people. For the Bushmen who lived formerly beside the Orange River, it was fire that drove the animals away from the shelter of the tree under which they and people had been sleeping together; and in the !Kung legend the irons ≠Gao!na used to brand the animals with their markings were heated in the flames of the 'eternal fire'.

In very ancient times fire transformed the life of the hunter, and today the Bushmen still value it with food and water as one of the three necessities of life. On cold winter's nights, the cupola of light fire casts above and around them is their comfort and their protection.

Although the accounts that Bushmen give of how people acquired the use of fire vary considerably from one locality to another, even those as different in all other details as the myths of the !Kung and the /Gwi have one common ingredient: a children's toy which the former call a *djani* and the latter call a *zani*. In the late afternoon at all the Bushman camps we visited, young boys with sticks dashed this way and that, leaping over low bushes in their effort to get directly beneath a *djani* drifting on the breezes as it floated down spinning from the sky. The boy who is under it when it comes within reach catches it on the point of his stick and hurls it back as high as he can, and the chase begins anew.

It is made from a 35 centimetre length of hollow reed, with the small, soft under-feathers of a guinea fowl stuck into one end and a short thong, weighted with a nut or lump of gum, fastened to the other with fine sinews. A larger feather, trimmed to symmetry by burning the edges with a glowing faggot, is similarly bound to the reed shaft slightly above the mid-point, curving outward to give the toy its spin. It is a plaything of great antiquity, for it was being made already in that far-off time when things happened which no longer happen today, and when all the animals were still people. Indeed, the /Gwi say that, were it not for the *zani,* mankind would still be living in darkness.

According to their story, Pisiboro one day discovered Ostrich eating berries in the bush. When Ostrich raised his arm to pick more berries, Pisiboro noticed the smell of burning which he traced to a hot coal that Ostrich kept hidden under his arm. Pisiboro said nothing, but, determined to expose Ostrich's secret, he contrived to meet him again in the bush next day, and then asked him to pluck some berries from one of the upper branches. When Ostrich reached up to oblige, Pisiboro snatched the hot coal from Ostrich's armpit, ran off with it and finally threw it at an antheap, where it shattered into small pieces. Then he told the fire to hide, and it concealed itself in the stones and in the branches of the brandybush, from which Bushmen have made their fire-sticks ever since.

Pisiboro then made a *zani,* using the wing of a korhaan for its feather and weighting it with a burning coal. Like small boys today, once, twice he flung it into the sky and it floated back to earth. Then he used a stick to hurl it a third time, and it flew so high that it remained there and became the sun. And so men have light and warmth, and every year the fire rises in the branches of the brandybush to ripen its fruit.

But the !Kung say that long ago there was a time when there was no fire on earth and all people ate their food raw. According to them one man, who was named /Ka /Kani, discovered the art of making fire by twirling one stick on another, and so he and his family ate cooked food. However, they did not share their knowledge with other people – until a chance visit by ≠Gao!na when /Ka /Kani was not home left them no choice in the matter.

≠Gao!na asked /Ka /Kani's children for something to eat, and they gave him cooked food. It was so delicious that he came back the next day for more. But as he approached he saw that /Ka /Kani was making a fire with his sticks, so he watched from a distance to see how it was done and how food was cooked. After noting where /Ka /Kani hid his fire-sticks, ≠Gao!na went into his camp as if he had seen nothing and joined in the meal. But his chief interest now was to lay his hands on the fire-sticks, and so, after they had eaten, he suggested that they play a game and, using guinea fowl feathers, he made two *djanis.* However, /Ka /Kani's *djani* did not fly high enough or drift far enough to draw him away from the place where he had hidden his fire-sticks. So ≠Gao!na replaced the feathers with bustard feathers, and the next time /Ka /Kani threw his *djani* it flew higher and took longer to come down. ≠Gao!na then caused a wind to blow the *djani* so that /Ka /Kani had to run a long way past him while chasing after it. Seizing his chance, ≠Gao!na dashed to the hiding place and, taking hold of the fire-sticks, broke them into small pieces and threw them into the air, spreading them over the whole world. As punishment for his selfishness, /Ka /Kani was changed into a bird, and since then people everywhere have cooked their food, for from that time there has been fire in every piece of wood.

The !Kung do not worship fire, but they respect what it symbolises in their social and spiritual lives by observing certain usages. A new-made fire represents their expectations and initiates a new period of possible good fortune for them. Thus a band dogged by misfortune will move elsewhere and kindle a new fire. Once they have abandoned such a campsite they will never return to it, for to light a new fire in an old fireplace would only lead to their resuming the ill-fortune which made them abandon the site.

But whether a band abandons a campsite because of misfortune, death or merely because they want to try a new place, the first act performed at the new campsite is the lighting of a new fire by the traditional method of twirling the fire-sticks.

We were once with a band that had just lost one of its senior members and we moved
with them to a new site less than a kilometre from their old camp. Tushay, who was the oldest man in the band, performed the ritual of lighting the new fire.

He took his fire-sticks from his quiver and cut a notch at the end of one of them. Then, holding it firmly on the ground with his foot, he fitted the tip of the other stick into the notch and began rolling it rapidly between the palms of his hands, exerting downward pressure at the same time to increase the friction.

The effort was evident in the muscles of his face and in his deep breathing, but in less than a minute the softer wood of the notched stick began to powder at the point of contact. Moments later the powder turned black and started smouldering. Tushay then tipped it onto some tinder and blew on it until it flared. He added kindling to the flame and, once the new fire was well established, the heads of the families in the band took blazing faggots from it to start their own domestic fires.

These domestic fires are at the heart of family life. It is not in their huts that the Bushmen live but at their fires, for hearth is home. They cook on them, gather about them to talk whenever their activities do not take them away from camp, and at night they sleep beside them, the women on one side, the men on the other. When the fires are not needed during the day, they are banked with ashes, so that the flames may be fanned afresh from the coals every evening. Throughout the night they burn with a small flame. The Bushmen do not want to be scorched by a roaring blaze in their sleep or smothered by thick smoke. Nor do they wish to collect and carry more firewood than is necessary. For them the mystique of fire lies not in the dramatic pyrotechnics of the bonfire, but in the warm glow of the household hearth.

Every nuclear family has its own fire, and related nuclear families position their fires close to one another, rather than live mingled with other families, but all the fires have their source in a single act of fire-making, and as in this sense everyone sits at the same fire, the fire is symbolic of the unity of the whole band.

Bushman nuclear families are necessarily small. The vicissitudes of their hunting and gathering fortunes cannot guarantee that there will be sufficient food to sustain a disproportionate number of unproductive members, while too many small children requiring to be carried could crucially hamper the women in their vital food gathering activities. These are survival considerations, and the Bushmen cannot afford to be swayed by sentiment. They love their children and indulge them to an extent that would be remarkable in Western societies. On the one hand they wish they could have more of them, but on the other they must be pragmatic. Their ideal, therefore, is to have three or four children spaced about four years apart. Low fertility and high infant mortality incline naturally towards this ideal, but when pregnancies do occur which could endanger the self-sufficiency of the family and the band as a whole, the Bushmen may 'throw down' a new-born child. The expectant mother goes off into the bush to have her baby and returns without it. Nobody comments. It is a subject that is never discussed. The freedom of the Bushmen is the freedom of necessity.

In former times, many missionaries and others who came from vastly more affluent cultures with the conviction that they were bearers of ultimate morality and absolute truth made no concessions to necessity and were so appalled by the Bushman practice of infanticide and the supposed practice of abandoning their aged to the hyaenas that they regarded them as less than human, while Bushman standards of superficial bodily cleanliness – the non-availability of water notwithstanding – were viewed as an offence against Victorian plumbing and, therefore, against God. The same critics, flushed with reverence for the sanctity of the monogamous bourgeois family, vociferated against the 'indolence' of the Bushmen for electing to live by the chase instead of 'honest labour' in the fields, and against the 'moral turpitude' of their matrimonial customs.

While Bushman marriage is polygynous in theory, and a few men do have more than one wife, the monogamous union is favoured as a general rule by the scarcity of women and the added demands which each additional wife makes on a man's prowess as a hunter.

The first test of the suitability of marriage partners is that wedlock should not violate the incest taboo, which extends beyond the immediate family to include other categories of persons between whom sexual relations, and therefore marriage, are not permissible, because they are deemed to be close kin, according to local usage. On the other hand, certain marriages that help alleviate communal problems, such as those to the widow or widower of a deceased brother or sister, and those which help strengthen ties between neighbouring bands, are especially favoured.

The first marriages are usually arranged by the parents, and among the !Kung a man may be betrothed while he is still a child. As the desired age difference between husband and wife may be from ten to 15 years, it is not out of the ordinary for a girl to be betrothed pre-natally. But parents do not force a daughter into a marriage she objects to strenuously. The mate they chose for her will not have been selected haphazardly, however, for they will have sought a man who will treat her well, above all, a man who is a good hunter. This is not only because they are concerned that he should be a good provider for her, but that he should also be able to provide adequately for them, as it is the custom that a young man goes to live with his wife's people after marriage and that he hunts for her parents and their dependants. This intimate connection between hunting and marriage is ritually emphasised at the time of the wedding, when the groom must present his bride's parents with an animal he has himself killed. A man's ability as a hunter is the measure of his manhood; his hunting powers earn him reproductive rights and so the band is strengthened and perpetuated.

Marriage, divorce and remarriage are not highly involved procedures, however, and a girl who discovers that her new husband is not to her liking may return to her parents' fire and thereby terminate the marriage. Many first marriages end in this way, without attracting strong public disapproval.

When the fierce south wind drives Bushmen into huddles over their fires on cold winter's days, the intensity of face-to-face relationships is stressed. In such small societies, where everyone is constantly inter-acting with everyone else, the potential for friction, discord and conflict is never far beneath the surface of apparent cordiality. Although the subsistence nature of their hunting and gathering way of life militates against one Bushman growing conspicuously more opulent than his fellows, little jealousies nevertheless exist and sometimes bubble to the surface. Real and imagined slights are nursed and, in times of tension, remembered – occasionally with fatal consequences.

But, between the germ of hostility and recourse to the poisoned arrow, Bushmen have evolved a series of safety valves, which are backed by the sanction of public disapproval. Among people who do not see it as the function of their gods to redress earthly wrongs and who lack a centralised temporal authority with power to restrain and punish offenders, the injured party must in the last resort take up arms himself to obtain satisfaction. Because this almost invariably means death, Bushmen have such an ingrained fear of fighting that they speak idiomatically of any traumatic experience as 'a fight'.

The safety valves, developed probably by a lengthy and not consciously purposeful empirical process, release tension in various ways before anyone is driven to seek ultimate satisfaction in violence. There is an underlying awareness that it would be impossible for them to pursue the hunting life as lone individuals or even as small, isolated families. Every individual depends on his band for his existence. Only through co-operation can all eat when only a few are successful. There are many vital tasks which one man cannot undertake on his own, and without the companionship of his fellows, a man lacks the sense of identity which he feels is necessary for his security and comfort. Thus the fear that he will

be disapproved of and rejected by the band constrains him to abide by its uncodified laws
and submit to its restraints.

The kinship system lies at the grass roots of their social order. Among some central Kalahari Bushmen, such as the /Gwi, who spend the greater part of the year dispersed in small family units over their territories, the system does not extend beyond the immediate family. However, among the !Kung, who congregate in larger numbers at their permanent waterholes throughout the long dry season, the system is so complex that every !Kung is able to address virtually every other Bushman he knows by a kin term. In each case, the term is accompanied by a code of appropriate behaviour that is so deeply ingrained in their way of life and so actively supported by public opinion that it is seldom violated. For instance, no hunter would think of refusing to provide his wife's parents with meat and skins, for this is unquestioned custom. Were he to refuse, he would be judged wrong by the band, and manifest public disapproval, even ostracism, would be his punishment. Among the !Kung the system is not confined to people related by blood or marriage but includes a whole category of 'name relatives' consisting of people who share the same name. There is an element of word magic in this, as if there were a mystical connection between people with the same names in which each participates to some extent in the identity of the other.

Closely bound up with kinship are parallel systems of what social scientists call 'joking' and 'avoidance' relationships. For each individual, everyone else falls into one of two categories: those with whom he may exchange sexual banter and sex-related insults, and those he must treat with formal respect. These relationships are treated as social axioms, and Bushmen derive security from conforming to what they know is proper behaviour. And so, every Bushman has a group of people towards whom he may be irreverent and insulting with impunity, knowing that they will not take offence, but will accept what he says as jest, even if many a true word is spoken. On the other hand, he also has a group of people towards whom he must be reserved in his demeanour. Hence in his daily life he is continually alternating between opportunities for letting off steam harmlessly and occasions for showing humility. And as all have both types of relationships, no one is subjected to the irritation of unremitting abuse or the tedium of purely formal contacts with other people. The balance struck between the two is a keynote of social harmony.

But the counterpoint of the two types of relationships cannot alone produce or preserve total harmony; other notes must be introduced to gloss over the discordant lapses. We saw clearly how the customary sharing of meat helps reduce tension, but this is assisted by other regularised practices, such as borrowing, lending and exchanging gifts, which operate in a similar way.

Bushmen need little in the way of material possessions. When a man has his weapons and his few implements, his skins and his utensils, what purpose can there be in duplication? What else should he own? Possessions do not make the man, so why encumber oneself with surpluses? As he is able to make a replacement easily for everything that he owns, the notion of private property is weakly developed. Little importance is attached to the thing itself. Instead, there is continual borrowing and lending which, apart from being one of the ways in which people are able to help one another, also establishes bonds between borrowers and lenders, for it would be foolish to quarrel with the man whose axe you are using, because you would have to return it to him. Since at any one time almost everyone is bonded to others in this way, the number of persons between whom friction is unlikely is substantially increased, and consequently fewer people are liable to fall out with one another at the same time.

The idea of committing oneself to maintaining pacific relations with others is more fully developed in habitual gift exchange, which creates bonds of goodwill and obligation which endure for longer. Bushmen say that gifts restore peace between people who have fallen out, and that to give someone a present is, therefore, about the best thing one can do. By the same token, to refuse a gift is an act of hostility. Great importance is attached to the regular flow of ostrich egg shells, artefacts, eland fat, beads, arrows, skins, knives and other gifts between members of the band. Everyone knows which objects are on the gift circuit, who owns them at present, who owned them in the past and whose hands they are likely to pass through before they reach him. He therefore cultivates the good graces of those who are before him on the routes of the presents he most covets, and once he accepts a gift he is under obligation to reciprocate with a gift of equal value. But he should not hasten to do so, lest he debase the exchange by making it look like trade. Thus weeks, and even years, may pass before a present is given in return. But if the giver of the first gift feels the recipient is taking too long to respond, he may ask what has become of his present. If he still fails to elicit a response, he airs his complaint by raising it repeatedly in general discussion.

Talking is the great Bushman pastime. Whether they are out in the field or sitting around their fires at home, they talk incessantly. Talk, laced with laughter, is the solvent of their tensions. It provides an outlet for emotions and a channel for conveying what they think and feel to others. While it is the soul of conviviality, it is also the most effective means they have of enforcing social discipline. Talk that is intended to correct misdemeanours may amount to no more than someone thinking aloud about a grievance or telling someone else about it within earshot of the offender in the hope of making him aware of his error and inducing him to change his ways.

N!aba was angry with Dam, her husband, because he no longer helped her collect firewood. Whenever she went to look for fuel, Dam was elsewhere talking to his friends and deaf to her entreaties. Dam also had a reputation for being quick-tempered, and so it was unwise for her to upbraid him to his face. So she told everyone else about his lack of consideration instead.

'How hard it is for a woman to be the wife of such a man,' she sighed loudly whenever he was nearby. 'What sort of man is it who sits about doing nothing while his wife must do such heavy work?'

Dam pretended not to hear her at first, but she kept it up until the other members of the band grew tired of her refrain. They knew that what N!aba said about Dam was true, and so they began to echo her words. When Dam realised that everyone disapproved of his behaviour and that even his closest friends were talking disapprovingly about him, he started going once more with N!aba to collect firewood.

When a major dispute threatens to burst into violence, it is confronted by the entire band in frank and forthright discussion, which leaves the offender in no doubt about the consensus of opinion concerning his behaviour and where it is likely to lead him. And then again, when their leisure is not beset with pressing problems, carefree banter and merriment wash over them in their dome of firelight, bathing them in the warmth of good companionship, flooding with their excitement and ebbing perhaps as the plaintive notes drawn from a four-stringed //gwashi plink like golden droplets into the surrounding pool of darkness.

Considering the central position that fire occupies in the domestic and social lives of the Bushmen, it is not surprising to find that it has the equivalent place in their ritual expressions of their spiritual concerns. The menarchial rite, the rite of the first kill, rite of a child's first haircut, rite of the novice medicine man and the major rites of the healing dances all have special fires as their focal point; ritual fires, which may not be lighted from the coals of other fires, but must be made anew each time with fire-sticks in the ancient way. These rituals are the Bushmen's links with the non-temporal world; with the forces of creation, death and transcendence.

Bushmen believe in the existence of two gods; a greater god and a lesser god. They have many names, but the !Kung Bushmen most commonly call them ≠Gao!na and //Gauwa, while to the /Gwi they are N!odima and G//awama. However, to observers whose eyes have been predisposed by a culture suspended between the promise of Heaven and the threat of Hell, they are the 'good' god and the 'bad' god, representing the duality of virtue and sin.

The missionary Campbell, who revealed much in spite of his inability to understand it, tried hard to extract definitions of 'good' and 'evil' from a young Bushman, and obtained for his pains no more than the assertion that it was 'good' to sleep with another man's wife, but 'bad' if he slept with yours. Still lamenting the Bushman's ignorance of absolute morality, he later asked the man, whom meanwhile he had discovered 'was in the habit of smoking wild hemp', what he thought was the most wonderful thing he had ever seen. The reply he was given, that no one thing was more wonderful than any other and that all the animals were the same, set him off on a homily deploring the incapacity of the savage mind for appreciating the wonders of God's creation, because it failed to discriminate between His creations. But then, Campbell's mind was filled at the time with fantasies of ships sailing up the (unnavigable) Orange River and of great industrial cities arising on its banks – an appropriate way of showing appreciation of God's creation, to his way of thinking.

But the stark duality that underlies the cultures of cities with police force, law courts, gallows and a God who rewards the 'good' with eternal life and punishes the 'bad' with perpetual damnation, is absent from the Bushman's view of himself and nature. The hunter, with his vast knowledge of plants and his empathy with animals, his identification with the rhythms of the natural order, discriminates not morally but pragmatically between fortune and misfortune, between what is beneficial and what is harmful, between that which gives him pleasure and that which causes him pain. And even in this pragmatic sense, nothing is wholly 'good' or wholly 'bad'. There are nuances between the white light and the deepest shadows. The opposites are not truly opposite, because each contains a little of the other, as in the Taoist unity of *yin* and *yang*.

≠Gao!na, the Great God of the !Kung, using one of his seven divine names, created himself, saying:

I am Hishe.
I am unknown, a stranger.
No one can command me.
I am a bad thing.
I follow my own path.

Then he created the lesser god, //Gauwa, naming him thus and giving to him six other divine names, reserving only his earthly name, ≠Gao!na, for himself alone. And so, as namesakes seven times over, they have a joking relationship, and the duality is resolved in the mystical participation that persons so related by name have in each other's identity.

≠Gao!na, tallest of the Bushmen, was in his earthly existence a great magician and trickster with supernatural powers, capable of assuming the form of an animal, a stone or anything else he wished, and who changed people into animals and brought the dead back to life. But as the Great God who lives beside a huge tree in the eastern sky, he is the source and custodian of all things. He created the earth with holes in it where water could collect; he created water itself, the sky, rain, the heavenly bodies, all the plants that grow and all the animals that feed upon them. He created people and gave to them all the weapons and implements they now have, and he implanted in them the knowledge of how to make all these things for themselves. Thus their hunting and gathering way of life was ordained from the very beginning.

≠Gao!na does not reveal himself to ordinary men, however, for so great is his power that, were he to come too close, he would destroy them unintentionally. But he nevertheless retains an interest in them. Although he is in no way concerned with their quarrels and the things they do to one another, he is aware of their actions, and if their behaviour offends him he will deal with them appropriately. But he is not truly a god of vengeance. When he deals harshly with someone, it is not so much an act of retribution as a demonstration of his power, which should be properly respected. This is the power of the unknown, the 'stranger', which explains why lightning strikes one man dead, and not the other standing beside him. The dead man, it is reasoned, must have offended ≠Gao!na by referring to him by one of his divine names, or perhaps he abused food.

But this is not ≠Gao!na's principal function. He is not continually on the look-out for offenders. It is only when they happen to come to his attention that he demonstrates his power, and so sometimes people do offensive things and get away with it. Chiefly he acts for the benefit of mankind, for he supplies men with rain, food, children and poison for their arrows.

//Gauwa, the lesser god, who lives between two great trees in the western sky, also performs deeds which may be either beneficial or harmful to man, but most are harmful. He is pictured as a very small Bushman, an incompetent who, even when well-intentioned, may bring misfortune by mistake. Although he is supposed to be subservient to ≠Gao!na and to act at his behest, he also sometimes acts on his own initiative while travelling about in a whirlwind, causing sickness and death to those he touches in passing. The people say that at certain times they catch glimpses of //Gauwa among the shadows of the trees.

The !Kung believe in an afterlife, in which their spirits become //gauwasi, who live in the eastern sky as servants of ≠Gao!na. As they see it, the spirit is not the same thing as life, which was placed in the body and kept there by ≠Gao!na, permeating every part of it except the limbs, which, as everyone knows, may be seriously injured or even lost without causing death. Life dies in the body and does not leave it, but the spirit survives, and the //gauwasi come to fetch it when someone dies, removing it through the head of the corpse and taking it to ≠Gao!na, together with the heart and blood of the deceased. These he hangs on a branch over a fire, and in the smoke, the heart, blood and spirit are reconstituted as a //gauwa (singular of //gauwasi).

As //gauwasi, they have eternal life. They age, but do not die, because //Gauwa renews them with a special medicine before they become too old. They have bodies, as they had on earth, and they have their own supplies of the same types of food they ate formerly. They also retain their former spouses, but eternity is a long time for even the best of marriages to endure, and so if any of them tires of a partner, he or she may cause a mortal woman or man to die in order to provide a replacement in the spirit world. This explains why a beautiful woman or an eligible hunter sometimes dies without apparent cause.

In such cases the //gauwasi are acting on their own initiative and in their own interests, although they normally serve as messengers of ≠Gao!na, bearing sickness and death as well as good fortune to humans. But because of the mischievous element in their behaviour, people avoid talking excessively about //gauwasi, as they do not want to attract attention to themselves.

The cloudless winter skies appear to be empty of all save the birds to the eyes of a stranger, but to the Bushmen the blue depths are webbed with invisible yet unbreakable threads on which the //gauwasi climb about the heavens. And at one point – some say it is at the Tsodilo Hills – one of these threads touches the earth and is the means by which the //gauwasi descend on errands for ≠Gao!na, with the miniature bows they use to shoot people with tiny arrows which may be felt but not seen, and from which those who have been shot eventually die.

To Bushmen, the death agony of humans is powerfully suggestive of the trauma of animals wounded by poisoned arrows. Thus the notion that men die because of wounds

inflicted by invisible poisoned arrows from the spirit world is also held by Bushmen other
than the !Kung. It is consistent with the symbolism of man the hunter.

Just as the isolation of bands has brought about a multiplicity of languages and dialects spoken by Bushmen, so too have the details of their beliefs been diversified. But the religious systems of all the Bushman groups that have been systematically studied contain the same suite of spiritual personages: a greater god, a lesser god and the spirits of the dead. Their roles may vary slightly. Sometimes one fires the 'arrows', sometimes another. Greater or lesser degrees of malevolence are attributed to their actions. For some the Great God is more remote than for others, but what he does and the order he has imposed on things are not to be questioned. Indeed, it is his nature to do as he does, and it would be presumptuous to ponder either his motives or his nature.

For Bushmen, the dividing line between the natural and the supernatural is not sharply defined, and what Westerners would call 'supernatural' forces are so active in the natural world of the Bushmen that the distinction between them is blurred. In so far as a duality does exist, it is transcended frequently by 'medicine men'.

But the state of transcendence is not the exclusive preserve of the 'medicine men', although they are more accomplished at attaining it. It is achieved by everyone who goes into a trance during the 'healing dance'. Many men enter a state of trance in this dance, which a band may perform as often as two or three times a week, as their principal means of warding off the ill effects of the arrows of the gods and the spirits of the dead.

Someone who achieves this state is said by the !Kung to *!kia*. This is a condition which is experienced rather than conceptualised, and it seems to correspond to the transcendental experiences which mystics emerging from the dogmas of many cultures in all parts of the world induce by a variety of disciplines and practices. Among the Bushmen, the medium is the dance, but the description they give of the inner physical process that produces the *!kia* state is strikingly similar to the way in which the kundalini form of yoga practised in India is said to operate.

The !Kung say that *!kia* occurs when a subtle energy, called *n/um*, is heated in the lower stomach region by the dance and rises up the spine as a vapour until it touches the base of the skull, at which point the energy is diffused throughout the body, like an electric current, causing the flesh to tingle and all conscious thought to cease.

People in this state are able to cross into the province of the supernatural and engage the spirits of the dead in battle on their own ground. A person charged with *n/um* repulses the spirits and is cured of his physical and metaphysical ailments, actual and potential. But *!kia* is not sought for selfish reasons. Those who attain it use it to cure other members of the community who fall victim to the arrows of misfortune. It would be a misuse of this power to keep its benefits for themselves. *N/um* energy is the universal 'medicine' which was given originally to man by ≠Gao!na and has been passed on from man to man ever since. All who can *!kia* are thus in this sense 'medicine men' and participate in the religious experience. But some 'medicine men' are more accomplished than others. Those who have absorbed a lot of *n/um* leave their bodies during the trance and ascend the invisible thread to visit //Gauwa in the western sky, and the greatest of the 'medicine men' sometimes even catch glimpses of ≠Gao!na himself.

There is no formal decision to perform a healing dance. It develops spontaneously from light-hearted singing and dancing that begins in the spirit of a game. But then, as more and more people join in, the emotional pitch rises, the dancers become more intense and, if the mood is right, it will develop into a healing dance that lasts until dawn.

We attended many dances on our travels among the Bushmen, but only very few of them became healing dances. No one could ever tell us if there would be a dance on any particular night. Often we were settling down for the night in our camp when the sound of singing and clapping drew us back to the encampment of the Bushmen with whom we had spent the day.

While we were camped in the vicinity of Tsumkwe, in the Bushmanland region of Namibia, we were attracted in this way to a nearby settlement three nights in succession. Each time we found a group of women and young girls singing and clapping around a fire. From time to time a few men joined in and danced within the circle of women. But nothing further happened and after an hour or two the voices became less lusty, the clapping less spirited and one by one the audience and participants drifted away to their huts.

On the fourth night we decided to ignore the sounds reaching us from the Bushman camp. We had already removed our boots and were zipping up our sleeping-bags when Tsamgao's young son, ≠Toma, and four of his friends came to tell us that Tsamgao said we should go with them, as there would be a dance that night.

We could sense a different atmosphere the moment we arrived there. Almost all the adult members of the band were gathered around the fire this time and the fire itself was larger and brighter than previously. Tsamgao was waiting for us outside the circle of participants. Though he had danced the healing dance many times, he said, he was unable to *!kia*. He would be a spectator with us and tell us whatever we wanted to know about the dance.

The fire, Tsamgao said, was specially lighted with fire-sticks, because no ordinary fire would be able to heat the *n/um* energy in the dancers and cause it to boil and rise.

The women and girls sat close to the fire, clapping and singing with rhythmic precision to stimulate the *n/um* in the men, who now began to dance round them in single file, stamping their feet in unison and shaking the strings of dried cocoons tied as rattles to their legs.

Voices, hands, feet and rattles combined to produce an intricate pattern of sound, which rose and fell in intensity. The flames cast a flickering orange light on their copper-toned features. The women held their hands high in front of their faces and gazed over the fire at infinity, while the men moved slowly in a line round behind them, stamping first their right feet, then their left and then both together, advancing only a few centimetres at a time.

It continued like this for about two hours without any change in the rhythm, but the participants seemed to have entered a timeless region of the mind in which nothing but the dance existed.

Gradually the dancers moved through a gap between two women and danced around the fire inside the circle. The singing and clapping grew louder, the tempo increased and the pattern became more complex.

Suddenly one of the men began to tremble violently, his eyes glazed, his face without expression, teetering on the brink of the trance. One of the older men moved towards him and tipped him over the edge with a snap of the fingers that represented 'fire arrows' being 'shot' into his stomach and spleen. The younger man collapsed into a trance.

Immediately the older men began massaging his stomach to prevent the 'fire arrows' from coming out and to work them gradually round to the back, so that when his spirit returned from doing battle with the spirits of the dead it would be able to re-enter his body.

The first man seemed to set the others off, because other men followed him into oblivion at frequent intervals. But after a while there came a longish period in which no one showed any sign of going into a trance, although there were still several men dancing round the fire.

At this point the older 'medicine men' left the line and began moving among the people, going from one to another, placing their hands on them to draw into their own bodies the 'wrong medicine' sent by //Gauwa and the //gauwasi and hurling it with curses into the darkness beyond the circle of firelight.

Then, as their fury reached a crescendo, they stopped healing and, seizing blazing sticks from the fire, flung them into the night, and shrieked challenges and imprecations at the incompetent and malicious spirits.

One of them staggered into the fire and rubbed hot coals over his body. And then he too sank into unconsciousness and was pulled from the ashes. His spirit had gone, Tsamgao said, to remonstrate with //Gauwa in the western sky.

The trance state is accessible to all Bushmen but fewer than half actually enter it, for the transition is described as 'half-death'. The sensation of dying is experienced when they must let go of their personal identity in order to be reborn in the experience of *!kia*. Many are unable to overcome their fear, but the number who do is remarkably high, considering how few attain transcendental states in other cultures. This is because *!kia* is not an esoteric doctrine reserved for the elect or a practice confined to a subculture; it is fully integrated into the social and spiritual lives of the Bushmen, uniting nature and supernature and bringing the whole community together.

Although the exact form of the healing dance is not the same for all Bushmen, it has a constant role in their lives, uniting the community in an ecstatic group experience as nothing else does, bringing them into harmony with one another and placing them in tune with the infinite.

Heaven and earth, water, fire, the plants that grow and the animals that feed upon them are linked to the Bushmen's own lives as hunters in a cosmological perspective in which even death has its proper place.

BROWN HYAENA IN THE SUN

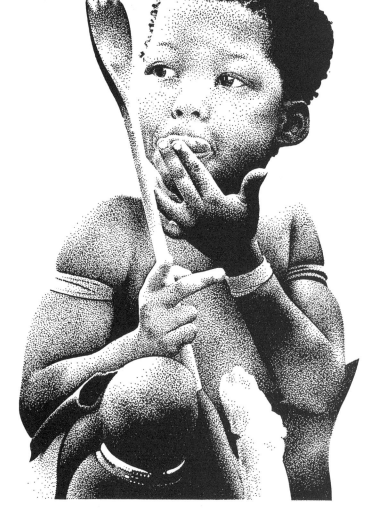

When a !Kung Bushman seeks guidance in the hunt or any other endeavour he turns to his divining tablets. Within the throw of these tablets he can discern events that lie in the near future, and each of the five tablets is given a name appropriate to the question it is meant to answer; names such as Earth, Water, the designation of an animal, Fire and Sun. But one of them is always called Brown Hyaena. This last of the animals created by ≠Gao!na is regarded as a 'death thing', because it is commonly associated with carrion. There is a Brown Hyaena in every set of divining tablets. When it falls upside down it tells of grave misfortune and death.

Earth and water, the game animals and fire are all 'life things', but the sun, like the brown hyaena, is a 'death thing', because it dries up the waterholes, grass, leaves and wild fruits, shrivels the roots and berries and scorches people who are unable to find shade. For this reason disputes between Bushmen and later immigrants to their hunting grounds have been over not only their water and food resources but also their shade trees, which the newcomers cut down for firewood and building timber. To deprive a man of his shade is akin to depriving him of sustenance, and so, among the !Kung today, the Morning Star, of all the heavenly bodies, evokes sympathy and pity, for it is fated to traverse the sky ahead of the sun and never to experience shade.

The old Cape Bushmen who inhabited the more temperate coastal areas regarded the sun in its more benefic aspect, as the provider of warmth and light, without which they would not have been able to see when they went hunting and gathering and the skies would have been permanently black as an overcast winter's day in the far south.

According to their story, the sun was once a man, living on earth at the same time as the 'early race', but not one of them. The light shone from his armpit when he raised his arm in the morning, and darkness descended when he lowered it in the evening. But, because he lived on earth, his light illuminated only the area around his own hut and gave no benefit to other people. One day, when it was particularly cold, an old woman remarked to another that it would be a good thing if the children were all to pounce on him while he slept and throw him up into the sky, so that he could shed warmth and light on all of them. Overhearing her, the children went and did as she suggested, telling him that he was no longer a man; that henceforth he would be a true sun. And so it has been ever since.

There is no gradual transition from the coldest season to the hottest in the regions inhabited by the Kalahari Bushmen. The months of September and October are dominated

by the sun. During the day everything is tortured by its withering heat. The air is dust dry and
from mid-morning until late afternoon it is impossible to hunt or gather, as the sand becomes too hot to walk upon. To escape the strong winds and driving sand, people sometimes scrape hollows in the ground, urinate in them to dampen them, and then lie in the relative cool they provide, sprinkling themselves with sand to reduce the effects of solar radiation, sharing their bunkers with the flies that gather in pestilential number in every sheltered place. For the Bushmen, a 'place in the sun' is not the favoured place it is in the English idiom but one in which they are exposed to a death-dealing force.

Many Bushman groups today tell a story concerning the origin of death which is essentially the same as the account given by the Cape Bushmen in historical times. According to this tale, man may blame his mortality on an ancient argument between the moon and the hare. It is said that, in the days when the earth was inhabited by the 'early race', Moon declared that, just as he was dying and being reborn repeatedly in the cycle of his phases, so too would people die and be reborn. But Hare, who was mourning the death of his mother, denied this, saying that his mother was truly dead and would not return. They argued for some time about this, but Hare insisted that when someone died he remained dead. Eventually, Moon offered to demonstrate his own cycle of death and rebirth, but Hare refused to watch. This so enraged Moon that he struck Hare in the face and split his lip. Hare retaliated by scratching Moon's face, leaving permanent scars. Completely losing his patience, Moon withdrew the offer of immortality and decreed that Hare was no longer a person but an animal, to be hunted, savaged and eaten by wild dogs. Henceforth, said Moon, all men would die and not return. And from that time the hare has been an animal with a split lip, and men have been mortal.

Death comes equally to Bushmen; regardless of all their earthly behaviour, all people share the same lot in the spirit world. The death of a young person is always regarded as the result of supernatural intervention, and the spirits of people who die young are greatly feared, for it is believed that they bitterly resent having been removed abruptly from the companionship of their family and band and will avenge themselves indiscriminately and attempt to capture the embodied spirits of former associates to keep them company. The spirits of people who have died in old age are not so much feared, because death is natural for the aged and they have had time to come to terms with it gradually. In fact, old people accept that in times of great thirst and famine, when their band is perpetually on the move in search of food, it may become necessary for the other members of the band to leave them behind, with no more than a fire to warm them and a circle of dry thorn bush to protect them from the hyaenas during what will probably be their last hours. But it is not as if they were abandoned utterly to their fate. Whether they stay behind or continue with the band, the choice is unlikely to alter their fate, except that, if they continue, their presence could be the cause of the whole band having to share it. If the others find food and water before it is too late to save them, some of the men return with supplies to fetch them. If not, the old people know how their end will come. The others, knowing it too, will never return to that spot, and neither will their descendants, until its deathly associations have been expunged from collective memory.

All places associated with death are left strictly alone. When someone dies, the body is buried in a squatting posture facing the Great God's home in the eastern sky, and all the personal possessions of the deceased are broken over the grave, so that people passing that way will recognise it as a grave and keep away from it. The campsite is then abandoned, and the band moves to another place and does not camp there again for at least two generations.

Over the past 80 years it has become a convention among popular writers to characterise the Bushmen as a 'dying race', the remnants of which are doomed to vanish from the face of the earth before the end of the present century. The image of a once resilient people finally sinking into biological extinction is powerfully emotive, but it is too specifically suggestive of physical death to represent precisely the present state of the Bushmen. The !Kung word for death means both physical death and serious misfortune, and it is in this wider sense of the word that it is an appropriate description of the Bushmen today, for the extinction they face is cultural. But death and rebirth are united concepts in the Bushman cosmology. It is their security in their age-old identity as members of small, independent, self-sustaining bands that is disappearing, and their pain is the agony of rebirth into a new identity, the form and content of which are as yet only dimly perceived.

The Bushmen, after a timeless existence that had endured many thousands of years, were eradicated from the lusher parts of the sub-continent and confined to the thirstlands, where the harshness of the environment, to which they alone were adapted, became their last line of defence against the incursions of more powerful peoples. Here in the arid regions, where the absence of surface water has been a bar to the mass influx of the cattle owners, the Bushmen have not been exterminated by a conqueror; their way of life has been subverted by the pressures of more affluent cultures.

Something of the deep discontent with their lot that emerged from their contact with other peoples and of the pain they experience in the transition that has been thrust upon them is contained in a story that was told by the Nharo Bushmen of the Ghanzi district in Botswana more than 60 years ago. Although it is clearly a story of fairly recent origin, it is set, as are all explanations of why things are as they are, in the days of the 'early race'. At that time, so the story goes, the Bushmen and the white men and all the cattle, sheep and goats were gathered together in one place. But a dispute arose between the Bushmen and the white men over who should own the cattle and small stock. The white men proposed a tug-of-war and provided rope to settle the issue. When the men began to pull on it, however, it broke, leaving most of the rope in the Bushmen's hands. 'There,' said the white men, 'you now have the rope. Go with it among the tsama melons and, while your women gather food, use it to trap the steenbok and the duiker. We will have the cows, the sheep and the goats. You will wear the skins of the animals you hunt, but we shall wear clothes and wrap ourselves in blankets when it is cold.'

Sixty years later there are but very few Nharo Bushmen who live the old nomadic life of the hunter-gatherer in the Kalahari; the bands have broken up; even the stories have been forgotten. Today, it is the turn of the !Kung to express their resentment in a story which is intended to account for the disparity of wealth between them and their black neighbours.

Black people have the cattle and crops, while they have only the bush foods and the wild animals, say the !Kung, because of the stupidity of an old man named Kara/'tuma of the 'early race' and they continually revile his memory for his costly foolishness. Kara/'tuma was a Bushman, but he had two brothers, the eldest of whom was a black man, while the youngest was white. But the Bushman had been first, and beside him the black and white brothers were like children.

While out hunting one day, Kara/'tuma came upon a cow in the bush. He had never seen such an animal before and was surprised that it did not flee from him. Nevertheless, being a hunter, he did not think of catching it and taking it home with him. He shot it, as he would shoot any antelope, except that it was far easier to shoot than an antelope. Later, however, he told his black younger brother about the strange animal, and his brother asked to be shown the place where the cows were grazing. When Kara/'tuma obliged, the black man said that such a tame animal should not be shot, but should be taken home alive, to see if it could serve any other useful purpose. Not long afterwards, one of the cows taken home by the black man calved and began producing milk, and he was able to bind the hind legs of the cow with a thong and obtain milk for himself. He took the milk to Kara/'tuma and

offered to share it with him, but the old Bushman said that he would be content to lick out
the pot after the black man had drunk his fill. And so the Bushman continued to be a hunter, while the black man could sit back and milk his cows.

On a later occasion, while Kara/'tuma was out hunting, he came upon a field of sorghum millet, but finding that the husks were unpleasant to touch, he set fire to the field. Afterwards he mentioned his discovery to his black brother, who went to see for himself. He tasted some of the roasted grains and found that they were good food, and so he took home some that had not been touched by the flames and planted them. This is why today the black people have milk and grain, while the Bushman must still search for bush foods and hunt wild animals. This is why the !Kung today blame Kara/'tuma for the fact that the Bushmen, who were first, are now last.

It is significant that in the Nharo tale it is the white man who gets the better part of the bargain, whereas in the !Kung tale the black man is the principal beneficiary of discoveries attributed to the Bushmen. These are facts of local history. Although the Ghanzi district, which is inhabited chiefly by Nharo, but also by /Gwi and other central Kalahari Bushmen, was nominally a sphere of interest of the black Tawana tribesmen living to the north of them, the first non-Bushmen who settled in the area were whites, who established themselves at Ghanzi in 1874. The settlement lasted only five years, however, and thereafter Tswana tribesmen from the east began making annual hunting and grazing expeditions into these parts in the rainy season, and traded tobacco, iron and European manufactured goods for skins, honey and beadwork produced by the Bushmen.

Later, after all of what is today Botswana was declared a protectorate of the British Crown in the late 1890s, the new British administration of the territory allocated vast tracts of land in the Ghanzi district to white cattle ranchers, and since that time the whites have been the dominant influence on the lives of the local Bushmen. But there is no comparable white settlement in the north-western regions inhabited by the !Kung, and here, as in the south-western Kalahari, it is black pastoralists of various tribes who have altered the lives of the Bushman hunter-gatherers.

Wherever there has been sustained contact between Bushmen and other peoples it has resulted in the disruption of the social life of the Bushmen, and, as in the stories, it is they, who were first, who have ended up at the bottom of a new social hierarchy. This is not because the Bushmen are inherently inferior, nor is it because the other peoples have deliberately set out to destroy their way of life. It seems instead to be the inevitable consequence of a clash of fundamental interests between societies which are driven by incompatible imperatives. The hunter-gatherers are organised for subsistence and are essentially conservative; the pastoralists and farmers are geared to the accumulation of wealth and are, from the point of view of economic sophistication, progressive. The Bushmen strive to maintain an equilibrium between their own numbers and the capacity of 'unimproved' nature for supporting them, while the black men are creating a productive base that will support a steadily increasing population and they must, therefore, conquer nature and have an expansionist attitude to territory. The new territory into which they expand is already occupied by the hunter-gatherers, whose subsistence base is destroyed in the process, and whose only alternatives are to find a menial place for themselves in the economy of the newcomers or resort to stock theft.

These are the same alternatives that history posed for the old Cape Bushmen a century and more ago. Both led to extinction. Stock theft had a simple logic for the Bushmen: if the cattle replaced the game, what else was there for them to hunt but the cattle? But the cattle-owners saw the situation differently. They did not understand the Bushmen's predicament, and even if they had, it would not have made much difference to the outcome. They too had a predicament; their way of life also had its logic: they could not afford to tolerate stock theft. Sometimes an amicable agreement was reached between a particular Bushman band and an individual stock owner, whereby they undertook to herd his stock for a share of the milk and a portion of the natural increase of the herd placed in their care. It was the sort of change in lifestyle that becomes irreversible. Within two or three generations they had lost their ethnic integrity as well as their cultural identity. Where there were no agreements, blood flowed on both sides, but Bushman blood flowed until there was none left to stain the soil.

Today, the self-help style justice of the wild frontier is something of the past. Now there are laws to stay the cattle-owner's trigger finger and others to send delinquent Bushmen to prison. Stock theft, a crime often committed under the compulsion of necessity, is still among the most prevalent of Bushman offences against the larger society that has enveloped him, but he no longer has to pay for it with his life.

In our own wanderings we paused on one occasion at a remote police post in Botswana to ask the way to a Bushman band we had heard was in the vicinity. Noticing a Bushman moving freely about the post, we asked the local inspector of police whether the man would be willing to accompany us as a guide.

'I regret that it is impossible,' said the inspector. 'He is an awaiting trial prisoner.'

'But aren't you afraid that if you let him walk around he will run away when you're not watching him?' we asked.

The inspector looked for a moment across the flat, barren land that stretched unbroken to the horizon in all directions, and shrugged his shoulders. 'Where could he run to?' he replied. The question was clearly rhetorical.

We wanted to know what crime he had committed.

The policeman sighed as if it were an old story and replied gravely: 'He ate somebody's donkey.'

An estimated 55 000 to 60 000 Bushmen are alive today. Of these, some 25 000 to 30 000 are in Botswana, probably no more than 15 000 in Namibia, 4 000 in southern Angola, 200 in Zambia and fewer than 25 in South Africa.

In Namibia, about 11 000 Bushmen work on white-owned farms, chiefly in the Gobabis district, from where many of the forefathers of the 4 000-odd Bushmen now living on the Ghanzi farms in Botswana came originally to escape from the white men. To begin with, the first farms at Ghanzi did not prevent the local Bushmen from continuing to live there in their time-honoured way. The farmers were not wealthy men; they did not have freehold title to the farms, did not fence them, could develop them only very slowly and made use of the natural pasture, which was not intensively grazed at that time. Thus the Bushmen could remain on the land, hunting and gathering and moving about as they had done formerly. The farms being so vast, it suited the farmers to have them there, where they could be employed periodically as cattleherders and labourers in exchange for food rations. This arrangement continued to serve as a bridge by which Bushmen could move gradually from one lifestyle to another up until about 30 years ago, when the farming block was considerably extended, the farms were surveyed and fenced and new, more competitive methods of livestock management were introduced, which made the Bushman cattle herder redundant. The Bushmen had finally been dispossessed of their land. No more than ten per cent of them continued in the employ of the farmers, and no longer as part hunter-gatherer, part herdsman, but as a wage labourer. A man and his dependants lost any right to remain on a farm if he ceased to be an employee. And so the vast majority became squatters and hangers-on, and, because their old subsistence food base was no longer there to fall back upon, many were, and still are, compelled to resort to stock theft to feed their families.

These changes have almost completely obliterated all vestiges of their old social order. They are no longer members of tightly-knit bands united by ties of mutual dependence, but live in unstable association with other paid labourers, without the benefits of the old system of restraints and obligations to smooth out dissent and reduce friction. The women, who formerly were the main food producers, must either rely entirely on their men for support, or turn to prostitution.

But despite their sometimes pathetic condition, the Bushmen living on the farms have no wish to return to the old ways of the hunter-gatherer, whom they look upon as being 'backward'. Gone for them are the days when no one laid great store by possessions nor strove to be better off than his fellows. They see themselves as 'new people'. There is no going back. They aspire, although hopelessly, to wealth and status, considering the possession of European manufactured goods as a mark of prestige. The age-old customs and beliefs are abandoned. These are the people who were left with the broken rope for snaring game when the white men claimed the cattle for themselves. Now there is no game for them to snare, and they no longer have any use for the rope.

Those who bewail the fact that the first are now last and the last first, whose fabled ancestor allowed his black brother to take the cows and the crops and asked not for a share but merely the privilege of licking out the cooking pot, are the majority of Bushmen in Botswana now. About 14 000 of them are attached to black pastoralists, some as servants, others with sheep, goats and sometimes cattle of their own, and yet others who are no more than squatters on the fringes of affluence. Most of them, however, stand in a relationship of client to black patron, performing in return for food and tobacco such services as caring for his cattle, collecting firewood, hunting, planting and reaping. Their position is similar to that of serfs, but without the connotation of abject servility. Although there were many instances of ill-treatment the relationship between client and patron is often close, with the client, in a long-established association of this kind, being treated as a member of the patron's family, often being allocated some land to cultivate for himself and some stock of his own that graze with the patron's herds and drink at his well. Bushmen still living in the old way generally enter this kind of relationship by undertaking to hunt on behalf of a cattle owner for remuneration in the form of tobacco and food. Then, as they become increasingly dependent on him, they move their camp closer to his village or cattle post and eventually give up the old way of life altogether.

Some ten years ago it was estimated that about 6 000 Bushmen in Botswana and slightly more in north-eastern Namibia were still living as full-time hunter-gatherers. Today, although there are no reliable figures to go by, there must certainly be far fewer of them, and there is probably not a Bushman alive who has not been touched and to some degree changed by contact with people from the world outside. Boreholes drilled by governments modify their patterns of movement, fences erected to prevent the spread of cattle diseases also bar the migration routes of the large game animals; farms, cattle posts and settlement schemes lure them away from the kind of lives they led previously. Prolonged interaction with black tribesmen has made them aware of the advantages of keeping some chickens, a few goats and perhaps a donkey or two. Dogs, unknown to Bushmen in ancient times, are now seldom absent from a Bushman camp. These creatures have modified hunting techniques and, in some cases, even altered the purpose of the hunt. Dogs give the hunter an added advantage over his quarry, which tips the delicate balance between hunter and hunted. A Bushman hunter-gatherer is exempt from the game laws if he hunts with traditional weapons. But a gemsbok held at bay by a pack of dogs is more easily speared to death from the flank by a nimble Bushman. The hunter may thus be able to kill more game than is necessary to supply the band with meat. He finds a ready market for the surplus among non-Bushmen who themselves must abide by the game laws, and so a commercial motive creeps into what was originally a subsistence activity. The pots on the cooking fires are of European and black African manufacture. A man will find it is easier to fashion a quiver for his arrows from a length of black plastic water pipe than to go through the whole process of preparing root bark for the purpose. The slightest contact with outsiders may produce the profoundest of long-term consequences in a society so finely poised between subsistence and death.

When 20 years ago Laurens van der Post wrote about the Tsodilo Hills in his *Lost World of the Kalahari* he invested them with a highly subjective mystique, transforming them into a place of spiritual significance and pilgrimage. Americans and Europeans began arriving at Shakawe after making the long journey to Africa with the single purpose of visiting the Tsodilo Hills. Although the Bushmen of the Hills had not been there at the time of van der Post's visit, they were not missed by the 'pilgrims', who bought Bushman beadwork and bows and arrows as curios and gave them pocket knives, cigarettes, lighters, items of clothing and other useful articles. By the time the flood of visitors had dwindled to a trickle, old /Gao and his band had grown accustomed to this new way of acquiring things. Although they continued to hunt and gather as of old, they also continued making curios as they sat around their fires and began taking them to Shakawe, where they sold them for cash which they used to buy factory-made blankets.

It was on one of these expeditions to the river that Gumtsa had been recruited to work for a contract period on the gold mines. Although he had kept his 'skin' and resumed his traditional way of life when he returned, Gumtsa had also acquired a weakness for white man's liquor. It is a weakness to which most Bushmen are prone and upon whom it has a devastating effect, as it always does on people who have not evolved social safeguards for keeping it under control.

This we discovered as a result of a sequence of events which began with our buying some of their curios and almost ended up by giving us an opportunity to witness the death of a man from the effects of arrow poison.

When we went to Shakawe to replenish our supplies, Gumtsa and two other Bushmen asked to accompany us, as they wanted to make some purchases with the money they had received for their curios. We drove to Shakawe on the Saturday afternoon and dropped the Bushmen after arranging where we would meet them to start the return journey on the Monday morning. However, when we arrived at the rendezvous on the Monday morning there was no sign of Gumtsa, and it was early afternoon before we were able to extract him, glassy-eyed and incoherent from a beer-drink, and mid-afternoon by the time we had finally settled him in the Land Rover and started back for the Hills.

The following morning he was missing from the Bushman camp, but we traced him an hour later to another beer-drink at a nearby cattle post and persuaded him to come with us. He was sober when that afternoon his cigarette lighter ran out of gas. We had noticed from the beginning of our stay at the Hills that Gumtsa's most prized possession was a disposable gas lighter that someone had given him, and we had speculated on what his opinion of modern technology would be when it no longer provided him with a flame. When this happened, we tried to explain that it was now useless and should be thrown away, and to soften his disappointment we gave him a replacement from our own stock of similar lighters. He would not throw the old one away, however, and insisted on making a present of it to his friend ≠Owe.

We slept in our grass hut that night, and at about three in the morning we were awakened by the sound of manic laughter outside, and moments later two spears landed in the space between our beds. It was Gumtsa, and both the laughter and the spears were intended to convey to us that he had not come with hostile intentions. He then squatted on the floor of the hut and launched into a diatribe against his friend, whom, he said, had stolen his fire. He had obviously been back to the cattle post and had indulged copiously. He was, he said, returning to his camp, where he would kill his friend for stealing his fire. When we realised

that he was talking about his cigarette lighter, we quickly gave him another, in the interests
of sleep in our camp and peace in his, and he immediately took his spears and disappeared into the thicket opposite without further complaint. We were amazed that the lighter should be of such importance to him that he could contemplate killing a friend because of it and equally surprised that he had been prepared to brave the 'hunting time of the snakes' and come two kilometres through the bush alone at the dead of night to resolve matters to his own satisfaction. We were astounded next morning when we went to the Bushman camp and, seeing that both Gumtsa and his wife were now sporting new cigarette lighters, realised that the entire performance of the previous night had been an elaborate subterfuge to persuade us to part with another lighter.

The climax to Gumtsa's bout of inebriation came only late that afternoon, however. We had arranged with the Bushmen to climb Mount Female by an obscure route in the cool of late afternoon. When the men came to our camp at about 1630 hours, Gumtsa's glazed eyes again betrayed his condition. We decided to drive to the foot of the ascent to save time and energy. The other Bushmen clambered into the back of our vehicle, but Gumtsa insisted on taking his usual pilot seat on the bonnet. We bounced along the rutted track for a while, Gumtsa just managing to retain his perch. And then, for no clear reason, he extracted his single poisoned arrow from his quiver and fitted it to his bowstring. At that moment he had no free hand with which to steady himself, and the next instant he was falling, tumbling head-over-heels on to the ground beside the vehicle, the bow and poisoned arrow under him as he fell. We climbed out, scarcely daring to look. But if the divining tablets had been thrown in the Bushman camp before they set out that afternoon, the Brown Hyaena had certainly not landed upside down. Gumtsa was sitting beside the track, a study in incredulity. His left hand was tightly clenched and he rocked gently forward and back, muttering to himself. Then he opened his hand, and there in his palm lay the poison-dressed arrowhead. The shaft had broken off in the fall, but miraculously the point had not pierced his skin. He must have seen it as a miracle too, for the next moment he jumped up like someone demented, hacking branches from the surrounding trees and heaping them on the spot where the spirits of the dead had touched him on the shoulder and then passed him by.

But for the Bushman hunter-gatherers there can be no last-minute deliverance. It is the season of the sun which is a death thing. The forces of change, whether welcome or not, cannot be resisted. The tablets have been cast; the Brown Hyaena has fallen upside down. But after death comes rebirth, although the footprints in the sands of the future will not be the same.

EXPLANATORY NOTES ON CLICKS

The Bushman speak perhaps the world's most phonetically complex languages; languages whose most distinctive feature is the many click sounds. Some explanation of how they are produced is necessary before the reader can begin to approximate these sounds.

The linguist Anthony Traill points out that each click has a number of distinctive accompaniments which yield between 20 and 85 distinct click segments for the different Khoisan languages.

Experts differ on the manner in which each of the various clicks should be represented. In the captions and text we have followed the example set by Lorna Marshall in *The !Kung of Nyae Nyae* (1976).

/

This is the dental click in which the tip of the tongue is placed on the hard ridge behind the upper incisors. When the tongue is pulled away, a short, gentle sound is produced similar to the Englishman's 'tsk tsk' when expressing disapproval.

≠

The front part of the tongue is pressed against the alveolar ridge (that section of the mouth where the hard palate begins to curve up to the soft palate). On release a sharp, flat snap is produced.

!

In this click, the tip of the tongue is pressed against the alveolar ridge to produce, when sharply released, a loud, popping sound.

//

In the lateral click, the front part of the tongue remains on the hard palate while air vibrates at the sides. The sound produced is akin to that used when urging on a horse.

Tiny figures in a vast landscape (1): a party of Bushmen file homeward from their waterhole in the acacia thornveld of the north-western Kalahari. The knife-edge survival of these hunter-gatherers depends on their intimate knowledge of nature and their own ancient skills.

Overleaf: Invisible from afar, inconspicuous from nearby, a Bushman camp blends unobtrusively into the dry, level expanse of the central Kalahari. These temporary shelters are fashioned from branches, bark and desert grasses of the immediate vicinity. No permanent scars deface the land when the Bushmen move away. Stripped by the elements and foraging animals, the flimsy structures quickly decompose into the landscape and grass reoccupies the clearing, leaving no trace that man was ever here.

3

5

4

Hearth, more than hut, is home for the hunter. His fire ensconces him with family and friends in a dome of light; it is his solace on cheerless nights and the centre of his domestic and communal life. At all times of day small groups form and reform about the fires (3) to chat, share thoughts, exchange stories and give comfort, to listen and learn. Children are not excluded from adult discussions. They are encouraged to share in the fellowship of all ages, and they grow up with a sense of belonging to a community. They learn to be attentive to the needs of others, like this small boy (4) holding a stick in the coals for a flame to light his father's pipe, which was then passed round the circle for all to enjoy.

While some sit talking around a fire beneath a spreading kiaat in Bushmanland, Namibia (5), other members of the band continue with regular camp chores. But towards evening all gather about a single fire to relax. Glowing in the light of a copper sunset, a baby who has been fondled, cuddled, teased and reassured by everyone all day, now returns to his mother's arms (6).

6

Men are the hunters, but it is the women who feed the band from day to day, for it is their task to gather the leaves and berries and dig for the bulbs, roots and tubers that make up the bulk of their largely vegetable diet.

On a dry winter's morning in the central Kalahari, a party of Bushman women and children (7) set off on a day's gathering expedition, armed with pointed hardwood digging sticks. Old Xaube (8) is the most experienced gatherer in this party. As a child she acquired her extensive knowledge of plants by accompanying her mother. Even children too young to walk go regularly into the veld with their mothers, and so here learn the basic survival art of gathering.

Digging is often heavy work. N≠isa (9), digs some 30 centimetres to unearth a small onion-like bulb (10), which will be pounded with pestle and mortar and then mixed with powdered meat.

Overleaf: Sitting on her heels in a bald patch of sand, Xaube examines a large *Cucumis kalahariensis* tuber she has dug with much effort; it is a major food plant and source of precious water in the late dry season. The heavy work is lightened by the Bushman's genius for transforming work into play. Unlike the men, who must hunt in silence, the women indulge in continuous banter and playful rivalry whilst digging. Breezes whisper over the dry plains, and women's voices, calling attention to their finds, tinkle in the silences.

8

9

10

Without standing water for most of the year, Bushmen in the central Kalahari must for several months at a stretch rely on melons, bulbs and tubers for moisture. A tell-tale three-pointed leaf, barely showing above the ground, was enough to indicate to this woman (12) where she would find a juicy *bi* bulb *(Raphionacme burkei)*. Gently scraping away the sand so as not to break the slender stem linking the leaf to its storage organ about 30 centimetres below the surface, she carefully removes the bulb and puts it into a pouch in her antelope skin kaross. Back at camp (13) she holds the bulb firmly on her digging stick with her toes, to keep it out of the sand, and shaves the pulp into a basin, using the sharpened edge of a dry stick as a knife. On its own, the juice of the bulb is milky and bitter, so she chews leaves of the *Aloe transvaalensis* and then of the *Terminalia sericea* (14) and spits them into the basin. When the three ingredients are thoroughly mixed, the aloe removes the milky discolouration and the terminalia neutralises the taste. Then, squeezing some of the mixture in her right fist (15), she directs a thin stream of clear liquid from the tip of her thumb into the cupped palm of her left hand and sucks it into her mouth.

15

19

Bushmen eat a wide range of plants. Of several edible species of *Grewia* berries, the most favoured are those of the brandybush *(Grewia flava)*. Consisting chiefly of a large, indigestible pip with a thin fleshy covering, the berries are generally eaten by Bushmen on the move, who swallow them pip and all.

When Bau spied a bush of ripe berries while on a gathering expedition (16), she paused to savour a few. Her three-year-old son, Dam, is a little disdainful, but baby Gumtsa has already acquired a taste for their slightly astringent sweetness, and apparently knows where to find them.

In the central Kalahari *tsama* melons are an indispensable source of water for animals and Bushmen alike. And when the year is particularly dry, the melons seem by some miracle to grow in greater profusion. In the better-watered parts of the north-western Kalahari, where the !Kung call them *tama,* they are not used for their water; the flesh is discarded and only the pips are eaten. When little /Khoa brought home some *tama,* her mother, Di//khao, sliced them open (17) and cast aside those which she knew from experience would be bitter. Imitated by her daughter, she picked out the pips of the palatable melons. Later these pips were ground in her mortar, together with some dried meat and pieces of giraffe fat that had been crisped over the coals.

Seeds of the baobab which, roasted over the fire are reminiscent of toasted almonds, are pulverised with fat and meat in the same way by N/aoka (18). Personal spoons, like the one put to good use by this man in the central Kalahari (19), are usually hand-carved from the wood of the shepherd's tree. Visitors to these parts often assume that they are modelled on spoons introduced from outside, but their use is widespread among Bushmen, who claim that their ancestors made such spoons long before the white man came.

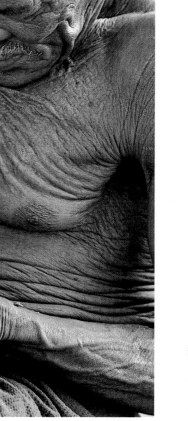

There is always something that requires attention in the Bushman camp, even if it is only baby Gumtsa's bottom that needs wiping (20), or Di//khao wanting her head shaved (21), to make her more beautiful and help combat bothersome parasites.

Their hands are constantly busy. Old /Gaishay (22) carves the sheath for a new 'Kavango knife', another man sews steenbok skins together to make a sleeping kaross (23), while N!ai finishes off an ostrich eggshell necklace (24).

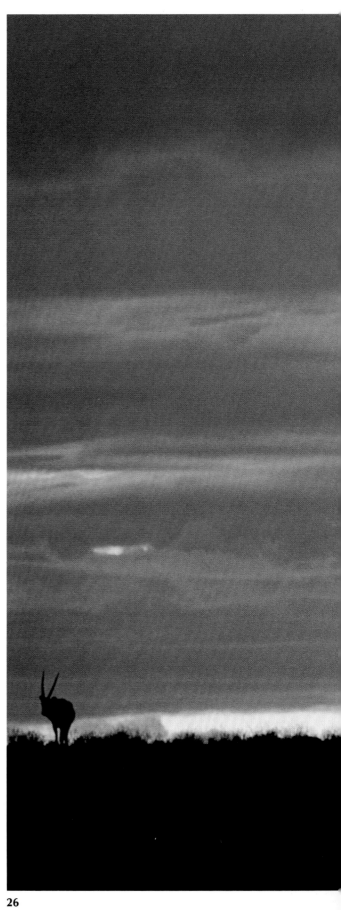

24

25 26

According to !Kung folklore, the black-backed jackal (25) was the last animal created and was given its distinctive markings, not by the Creator, as other animals were, but by contemptuous Bushmen, who burnt its back with the contents of a cooking pot. It is nevertheless regarded as a cunning and resourceful animal. It is common throughout the Kalahari, where we often saw it watching from a short distance for an opportunity to scavenge. Among the favourite targets of Bushman hunters, gemsbok (26) graze silhouetted against a threatening sky early on a spring evening in the central Kalahari. When the rains do come, they are capricious – passing by one area year after year, briefly visiting another.

A flock of ostrich stride out across a dune valley (27). The ostrich is hunted and eaten, but is difficult to stalk and its eggs feature more prominently than its flesh in the Bushman diet. In many bands the eggs are reserved by taboo for young children and elderly people. When these hunters discovered a nest, they first removed one of the eggs and watched to see whether another would be laid to replace it. When they were sure that no more eggs were to be gained in this way, the eggs were collected (28). Each of them was shaken, and those that had chicks developing inside them were returned to the nest. The rest were wrapped in grass and transported back to camp (29).

27

28

Old N!oshay prepares an omelette from one of the ostrich eggs, which is equivalent to about two dozen hen's eggs. After tapping a hole in the crown of the egg, she inserted a twig and twisted it to hook and extract the amnion membrane, which she discarded. She then scrambled the contents of the egg by twirling the twig in the aperture and emptied the liquid into a tortoise-shell basin, from which it was then poured into a shallow depression in the ground that she had lined with hot coals (30). N!oshay built up the fire around the depression, so that the flames would harden the top of the omelette. When it was thoroughly cooked, she dusted off the ash (31) and, after cleaning the underside, shared it with her friends.

33

34

35

Bo deepens his band's waterhole at N/ausha, in eastern Bushmanland, to over four metres, basining the bottom (32) so that the seepage will form a small pool. !Kung bands live near their waterholes throughout the dry season. This waterhole, says Bo, is temperamental, 'like a woman', because you never know in what state you will find it when you return.

Here women fill ostrich eggshells at the waterhole (33).

The /Gwi move widely over their territories during the dry months and for them water supplies are even more precarious. They cache ostrich eggshells filled with water along the routes they will have to travel in drier times; others are stored in the camp, propped around the inside of hut walls. Personal emblems denote ownership of the container and its contents, safely sealed with a grass plug. While the /Gwi emblems may represent snakes, birds, animals or humans (34), the !Kung carve only geometrical patterns similar to the designs on the shells this woman (35) is packing into her kaross.

Previous page: Completely engrossed in his task, Gumtsa hones the blade of his spear, while Xama, his wife, threads beads for a headband. Gumtsa's face and build reflect several typical Bushman characteristics. He is a small, slight man, compactly muscled and lithe. The golden-hued complexion, high cheekbones and slanted eyes of the Bushman led many to believe that they were of Mongolian origin. This has been disproved but nonetheless the Bushman has a singular appearance that distinguishes him from southern Africa's other indigenous peoples. Geneticists have shown that the black man and Bushman spring from the same stock – indeed, that the Bushman is closer to the prototype.

(37) A solitary shepherd's tree on a dune crest in the dying moments of the day, epitomises the loneliness of the Kalahari.
(38) At nightfall the world of the Bushman shrinks to the circle lighted by the glow of his fire.

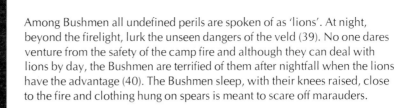

Among Bushmen all undefined perils are spoken of as 'lions'. At night, beyond the firelight, lurk the unseen dangers of the veld (39). No one dares venture from the safety of the camp fire and although they can deal with lions by day, the Bushmen are terrified of them after nightfall when the lions have the advantage (40). The Bushmen sleep, with their knees raised, close to the fire and clothing hung on spears is meant to scare off marauders.

Overleaf: Tree trunks haunt the mist and bushfire smoke drifts over a plain in southern Bushmanland on a frosty morning.

42   43

44

Bushmen find countless uses for string and rope they make from the fibres of a long-leafed species of *Sansevieria*. From the bundle beside him (42), /Qui, watched by his small son /Toma, takes one leaf at a time and separates the fibres from the green succulent tissue by drawing it repeatedly under the edged point of his digging stick. To make a single strand of his cord, /Qui rolls an appropriate quantity of fibre on his leg (43). He then twines two of these strands together, giving them a reverse twist, to produce a strong two-ply cord (44), which he uses for a noose snare. He hopes to catch a guinea-fowl and so baits his trap (45) with a small bulb which he knows these birds relish.

45

46

47

Bushmen have so perfected their snaring and trapping skills through countless generations that they scarcely ever fail.

After discovering the egg of a kori bustard in an unattended nest, a party of hunters sneaks back the next morning and sets a snare for the hen while she is out foraging (46). They peg out the noose on the ground near the nest and conceal it under a light covering of sand and leaves. The free end of the cord is tied to the tip of a springy sapling, which they anchor firmly in the ground at the other end and flex, so that it exerts constant pull on the cord. They then make a low fence of sticks in a wide circle around the nest, leaving only one opening so that the bird is forced to step on the hidden noose.

Being a bird with a marked reluctance to fly, the hen comes striding back through the grass, is diverted to the sole entrance and over the snare. As her foot touches the trigger mechanism in the centre of the snare the tension is suddenly released, the sapling whips back and the noose tightens with a violent jerk around her leg. It is a very indignant kori bustard the Bushmen find struggling at the end of their cord when they return late in the afternoon (47). A swift blow with a digging stick ends her struggles, and the men gather round to examine and discuss her (48). According to !Kung folklore, the great wings of the kori bustard fanned the flames of the Eternal Fire to heat the irons used to brand the animals with their characteristic markings.

(49-53) Women of all ages love to adorn themselves with beadwork and spend their leisure time in camp threading necklaces, bracelets, anklets and pendants, and working beaded designs on their karosses and leather aprons and into their hair. Traditionally, the only beads they had were those they themselves made – and still make – from ostrich eggshell. These they fashion by breaking the shell into many small pieces and then drilling a hole in the centre of each one with a tiny awl. To finish the beads they are held against the thigh, and the rough corners filed with a stone until they are all of similar size and remarkably regular shape.

When trade beads were first brought into their area, Bushman women had a strong preference for white beads, but vivid colours have become a passion.

54

(54) A living ornament, a butterfly rests on a smooth flank. (55) An old man's feet sculpted by lifelong contact with the hot sands of the Kalahari.

Overleaf: Suspended in mid-stride, springbok streak across a dune valley as they catch the scent of approaching Bushman hunters.

Deadly beetle larvae dug from the sands of the Kalahari are the foundation of the Bushman's whole way of life: the basis of his arrow poison and the ultimate deterrent. They are unearthed amidst an aura of magic from beneath certain marula and commiphora trees whose whereabouts have been known for generations.

Three days' walk from camp, Tushay and Bo (57) use their digging sticks to unearth poison. Apart from the crunch of the sticks in the desert sand, the silence is broken only by the nasal snorts uttered by each hunter in imitation of a gemsbok each time a larva is dug up.

The hunter may store the larva for several months cushioned with down in a horn container or in the 'cotton-wool' protection of a penduline tit's nest. When needed the fragile, earthen cocoon is carefully broken open and the larva removed (58) and its body juices squeezed into a small mixing cup fashioned from an eland or giraffe thigh-bone socket (59). Various plant ingredients, some of which are chewed and spat into the cup (60), are added to give the mixture further special qualities. One stimulates the heart, another causes local irritation, and both speed up the diffusion of the poison through the body of the animal.

Dressing the arrows is a ritual carried out with great care. In a specially cleared area, a little away from the centre of the camp, the hunters make a small fire around which they sit and work, each in turn relating the events of past hunts or expressing the hope that these new arrows will bring the same success in the future.

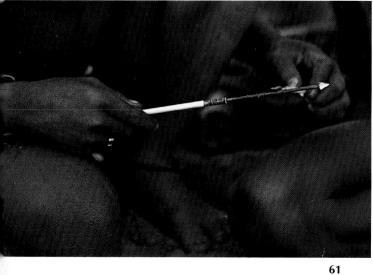

61

62   63

Poison mixture is applied to the sinew-bound portion of the steel arrowhead (61 & 62), not to the tip itself, otherwise even a scratch could easily prove fatal if an arrow slips in the excitement of the hunt.

After receiving their coatings of poison the arrows are laid to dry near the fire (63). Here /Tuka, Bo and Tushay have invited the teenaged Khan//a to join them and learn this vital hunter's art. A few days later the youth shot a giraffe using one of his own arrows but lost his prey due to his as yet inadequate skill at tracking. Arrow-poisoning is one of the very few activities from which Bushmen exclude their beloved children – the risk, they say, is too great to permit little hands to explore such dangerous things.

The hunt has begun. /Gishay, Bo, /Tuka and Tushay cross a dry pan in search of eland (66) which they know to frequent a nearby salt lick. Born and raised here, Bo knows every big tree and pan by its individual name, and through inheritance holds hunting rights to the area. Though his fellow hunters are from other areas, Bo accords them the same rights as himself while they hunt with him.

Once they sense that they are near their prey the men walk in silence, using only hand signals. Tushay indicates that there are giraffe ahead (64); there is a pause whilst fresh gemsbok spoor is examined and discussed in mime (65). The spoor tells them that it is a large female in calf and walking slowly, but they decide by consensus to try for the giraffe.

64

65

The hunters make for cover (67) as they silently approach the browsing giraffe, now only 80 metres away. One twig or leaf snapped underfoot and all would be in vain. Through a gap in the foliage Tushay aims an arrow (68) at the nearest animal while behind him his companions wait, bows at the ready, for a possible chance to shoot through the same opening in the vegetation. Hearts beat faster as the tension mounts, but this is the time for steady hands, when body and mind must be in total harmony if the skills acquired over a lifetime are to be used effectively.

67   68

Still unaware of their danger, the giraffe continue browsing. They seldom present such an easy target for the hunter.

70

71 72

The hunt is over and a fully grown giraffe lies dead, barely two hours after being shot. The animal could have taken days to die, but in this case the fatal shot – fired by Bo – penetrated the belly and quickly took effect. Once the animal began to weaken, the other hunters were able to score hits, too, entitling them to a good portion of the meat.

With a thorough knowledge of the giraffe's anatomy and the function of each of its organs, the hunters are skilful butchers and eagerly set about cutting up the carcass (70). The arrowheads are cut out and examined to establish ownership (71). The bent tip (72) of one of /Tuka's arrows illustrates what happens to these light projectiles when they strike something as solid as a rib. After three hours of hacking and cutting the hunters have enough meat to feed the band for several weeks (73). Bo uses one of the giraffe's stomachs to make his wife a blood pudding of which she is particularly fond (74). As the day nears its end, the hunters set off for camp (overleaf) with the first of several loads of meat that will be shared out by Bo and then subdivided again and again to everyone's satisfaction.

76

78

For the Bushman, to share means to survive. Alone in the Kalahari a man would soon perish, for he would have no claim to the waterholes, no one to assist him on the hunt, no collective wisdom to draw upon and no social fabric to allay his loneliness and fears. In the sharing of meat the interrelationships and obligations between men find expression, and so, when the hunters returned, they divided the meat in such a way that every member of the band received a fair share. Everyone knew what portion and how much of the meat they were entitled to.

Bo, whose arrow struck the giraffe first, made the first division (76) while the other men waited their turn. The meat that could not be eaten immediately was cut into long strips and draped over bushes to dry, out of reach of hyaenas, but when rain threatened, the drying strips were bundled and tied with giraffe skin and stored inside (77). The couple who received the intestines carefully cleaned them before hanging them up to dry (78).

Bo was entitled to a favoured portion and he took the head, which he buried in a pit filled with coals and left there to roast all day. When it was ready, he uncovered it (79), split it with his axe and shared the brains with his family.

Not only the Bushmen fed on the giraffe. Bo insisted that some of the less edible portions be left at the kill site for the brown hyaena (81) that came after dark to tear at the remains of the carcass. At dawn a handsome bateleur swooped in for what was left of the pickings (82).

Overleaf: The !Kung say that this baobab in Bushmanland owes its strange shape to its being contorted with pain when wounded by a porcupine quill while it was young.

When the last of the giraffe meat was eaten, people began accusing Bo of being wasteful, because he had insisted on leaving the foetus found in the giraffe for the hyaenas. Eventually, angry words led to blows, and for almost two hours the men grappled with one another. The spectators showed no alarm, but they wisely removed all bows and poisoned arrows from the scene. It was better, they said, that men should fight it out harmlessly in the open while their blood was up, rather than allow their grievances to fester.

The fight in the afternoon did not resolve the conflict and, in its aftermath, there was tension in the camp. Such discord among the individuals of a tiny band, whose very survival depends on co-operation, cannot be endured and that night the men began the 'healing' or 'trance' dance.

Bo took the lead and began moving slowly round the fire; one by one the other men joined him. The women sat in a circle singing and clapping, their clear voices and urgent rhythms spurring on the dancing men. Eventually some of the men attained that altered state of consciousness, the trance. In this state they are believed to be able to cleanse the group of discord and illness.

The old medicine man, /Gaishay, circled the fire only twice, then kneeling beside it, he plunged his head into the glowing coals (85) and held it there for some ten seconds. Rejoining the dancers, he moved among them helping them enter the trance state. As each man fell into a trance, others dragged him away from the fire and pulled the tip of his tongue out of his mouth so that he would not choke. Then he was left lying in a trance for about 20 minutes (86) before being massaged back to consciousness.

The next day /Gaishay showed no sign of injury besides a few singed hairs, and there was harmony in the camp.

Today, dancing and music are the Bushman's chief forms of artistic expression. Although the trance dance has social, religious and ritual significance, some dances are performed solely for pleasure.

To prepare for the trance dance (87), the men attach to their legs strings of rattles made from special dried cocoons and tiny chips of stone or ostrich eggshell. These make an insistent swishing sound as the men dance in a tight circle about the women.

Although the trance dance is the preserve of men, in other dances the women also take part.

87

88

Previous page: Bushman healing ranges from the dance to treatment that relies heavily on ritual and suggestion.

After a long period without meat Kgototxe, a /Gwi Bushman, killed a large antelope and ended his band's meat famine. To ensure his continuing success, he submitted, silent and unflinching, while his wife, Xhannakadi, pinched the skin of his forehead and made a series of small incisions with a sharp sliver of metal. After each cut, she removed the blood with two grass stalks and checked the bleeding with a smear of ointment made of fat and sweet-smelling powdered herbs. Then she took the bloodstained stalks and threw them to the winds, first to the south of their camp, and then to the north.

When /Gishay found himself unable to hunt because of a painful shoulder, he asked a medicine man to remove the 'bad blood' that he believed was the cause.

The medicine man made a number of incisions in /Gishay's cheeks and back (92 & 94) with the point of a poisoned arrow, careful not to allow the poison on the shank to touch the wounds.

He then placed blue wildebeest horns over the cuts, and sucked the air out of them through small holes at the points, which he sealed with a sticky resin gathered by bees (91). After a few minutes he pierced the seals with a thorn, removed the horns and poured out the clotted blood that had been drawn into them from the wounds.

The Bushmen smoked dagga (*Cannabis sativa*) long before they became acquainted with tobacco. Here !Kangwagai smokes it in a traditional ground pipe. Placing a hot coal on a wad of dagga in the underground clay pipe bowl, he filled his mouth with water and drew deeply on the narrow mouthpiece of bark, drawing the smoke through the water and into his lungs. Then he exhaled the smoke and spat out the water at the same time (93) and lay back with a contented smile while others had their turn.

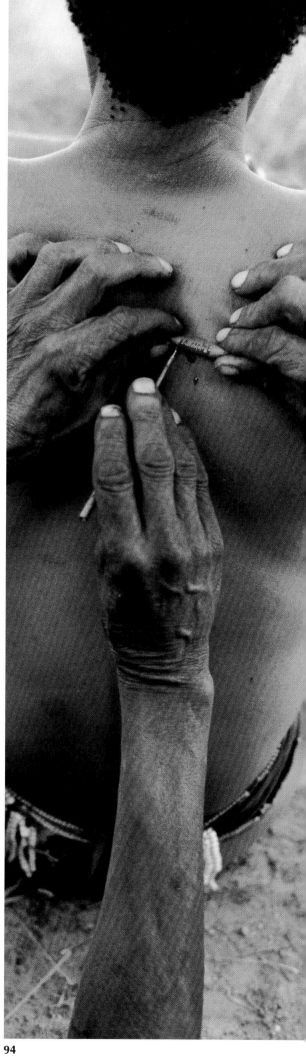

92

93 94

Old /Gashay, whose jaw had been disfigured in an early encounter with a leopard, was so old that he remembered seeing a black man for the first time only after he was married. Up to two years before, he had been the nominal 'owner' of his band's territory at N/ausha but he was now too frail to fend for himself, and the role had passed to his eldest son, Bo.

Now his people saw death in his eyes. They moved him to a temporary shelter outside their camp and began withdrawing emotionally from him, freeing him for death.
He spent most of his time sleeping in his shelter. One afternoon, a week after these photographs were taken, he dozed off for the last time.

To hear Bushman music is to encounter music anew. The delicate notes and intricate melodies, whether they are plucked from a five-stringed //gwashi of male mangetti heartwood (97), drawn from a simple mouth-bow (98) or produced in a tinkling duet of thumb pianos (99), haunt the senses.

Story-telling in the realms of folklore and legend is dominated by the older members of the band whose skills seem to evolve with age. With few exceptions the older people are master story-tellers and for hours at a time they keep their audience spellbound, skilfully interweaving themes and dramatising tales that have passed from generation to generation (102).

In their ordinary lives the Bushmen are all extremely voluble and articulate, and they love to tell and retell stories of their experiences. ≠Toma relates his favourite: how, when he was younger, he was attacked by a buffalo and rescued by a farmer.

103

104

The Bushmen we met at the Tsodilo Hills built us a hut. To make provision for our greater height, it was bigger than the shelters they build for themselves.

The men began digging elbow-deep holes in a circle at roughly equal intervals (103) as sockets for flexible poles (104), which they placed so that the natural curve in the poles inclined towards the centre.

Gumtsa (105), who directed the whole operation from the start, then bound pliable branches around the structure, lashing them to the uprights with strips of knobthorn bark. These horizontals strengthened the structure and preserved its shape. To complete the framework, everyone helped pull the tips of the uprights to the centre and bind them together (106).

The women went out to cut the grass for the thatch but the men helped carry it back to the camp (107). Thatching is also women's work. They bound bundles of grass to the framework in overlapping layers (108) while, inside, the men reinforced weak spots in the timbering (109).

107   108

109

For several months of the year water may be in critically short supply for many of the Bushmen but when it rains and the pans fill, the children revel in its plenty.

The people of the Kalahari thirstlands structure their lives around water. The !Kung tend to live close to their waterholes through the long, dry months and when the desert is refreshed by the rains, spread out across their territories. In contrast, the Bushmen of the central Kalahari move for most of the year from one group of food plants and moisture-filled melons and tubers to another but tend to gather around the pans during the rainy season.

Bushmen have a great love of children and they often say that their greatest sorrow is that the Great God gives them so few.

Baby N≠isa's smooth creamy complexion contrasts with //Kushay's wrinkled skin, darkened and creased by years of exposure to the Kalahari's harsh seasons and long nights spent close to the open fire.

Bushman babies are exceptionally alert and physically advanced compared with Western infants of the same age. Many of them walk well before they are a year old and they are endlessly encouraged to do so (116). When tiny Gumtsa succeeded for the first time, young Kanha in delight held him up for all to see (117) and soon he was back on his feet (118).

Childhood for the Bushman is a time of indulgence and freedom from care. When very young they are continually passed from one reassuring pair of arms to another, and they grow up with warmth, time and attention lavished upon them by everyone in the band.

116

119 **120**

A man who has not killed an animal with a bow and arrow remains a child, and from an early age Bushman boys begin to acquire the skills that will ensure that in their time they too become men.

When the youngsters came across an ostrich and her chicks they drove off the mother and played with the chicks, fondling and examining them, learning at first hand (121 & 124).

But they already know that there is no room for sentimentality between predator and prey. As their play became more boisterous, the chicks tried to escape and the boys, their hunting instincts quickly aroused, ran them down and killed them with sticks and stones (122).

Hunting successfully with a bow and arrow requires careful coaching and the boys are often taken into the veld by an experienced man (123). Whatever they manage to catch is taken back to the camp to add to the cooking pots. Here a small boy takes home a black korhaan hen (125).

121

122

123

124   125

126

127

Bushman bands are traditionally small and as a result the children play together regardless of differences in age. A traditional game among !Kung children is *n≠a n≠a hau* (126), which takes its name from a species of thorn tree. Hooking their right legs together, the children clap and sing as they hop round and round until one of them overbalances.

Khodo!kwangwa (127), a double-jointed /Gwi boy, entertains his fellows with his contortions.

The *djani,* with which according to legend light was brought to the world, is fashioned from reed, guinea-fowl feathers, sinews and gum. Using sticks, the children flick it high into the air (128). Then, as it spins slowly to earth, they dart beneath it to catch and flick it up again.

Inspired by the sight of his elders hunting giraffe illegally on horseback, Obi has made himself a horse and rider from two balls of dry dung (129).

Their only security their knowledge of the environment, a band in the central Kalahari travels confidently over the seemingly featureless landscape (130). For ten months of the year these Bushmen are on the move, shifting from one area of food plants to another, relying on the moisture of bulbs and tubers for most of their liquids.

Such an existence precludes carrying any non-essential possessions. Besides the tools needed for hunting and gathering, fire-sticks are a vital element in the Bushman's security. At night when temporary camps are set up (131), the tiny fires provide a focus for human companionship.

Overleaf: An oppressive pall hangs over the bushveld as the dry air fills with acrid smoke.

133   134

For many of the !Kung Bushmen who live in the relatively more hospitable north-western Kalahari, the mangetti nut (*Ricinodendron rautanenii*) is a staple food. At the end of the rainy season they converge on the great white dunes that are capped with groves of mangetti trees to harvest the nuts rich in oil and protein.

In a good year the nuts lie thick on the sand. Nuts still in the trees are dislodged with a well-aimed stick (133). Bushmen waste no energy, and nuts that are widely scattered are nimbly picked up with the toes (134), passed to the fingers and added to the women's bulging karosses (135).

There are no stones in mangetti country, but for the stone hammers and anvils that Bushmen through the ages have brought with them to crack the tough shells (136) and have left behind in the groves when they departed.

Although the Bushmen are slender and often even thin, their basic diet of nuts, fruits, berries and meat keeps them well-nourished.

Overleaf: The year before he died, old /Gashay was still able to walk the 70 kilometres from Tsumkwe to visit the mangetti grove he had visited each year since his birth.

135   136

On their way back from the mangetti grove to Tsumkwe, the band
visited a broad belt of spiny jelly melons (*Cucumis metuliferus*).
Bau (138) and the other women filled their karosses with over 200 of
this fruit, its remarkable flavour reminiscent of cucumber and
watermelon. The melons were roasted in a pit lined with coals (139)
and deep into the night the Bushmen feasted.

/Gishay climbed a monkey orange (*Strychnos cocculoides*) tree and shook its upper branches violently to dislodge the ripe fruit (140). The green and gold orbs which, despite his exertion, still clung to the branches, he struck down with a long stick.

Before carrying their haul back to camp, he and /Gao paused for refreshment. With their digging sticks, they cracked the ripe woody shells and they used smaller sticks to lever into their mouths juicy portions of the deliciously tart inner flesh (141).

While the Tsodilo Hills Bushmen were building our hut, 'monkey orange time' replaced our usual tea time, with old //In showing us how (142).

140

141

142

Shadows lengthen in the camp of the Tsodilo Hills Bushmen at the foot of Mount Male (143). Old /Gao (centre), told us that the mountain had once been a man, who had been turned to stone because he had not been able to live in peace with his wife. The large crack in the rock face, he said, was the scar where the man's wife had beaten him over the head.
Night closes in swiftly around the hunters after the sun goes down on the flatlands (144).

In the evening the Tsodilo Hills women draw water from a tiny pool fed by a seep inside a crevice in Mount Male. Xama crawled into the crack and used a monkey orange shell as a dipper to fill her gourd.

Long ago, Bushmen in many parts of southern Africa lived in caves and rock shelters, leaving beautiful animal paintings on the walls as evidence of their occupancy.

Today, the Tsodilo Hills Bushmen are the only Bushmen still to be found in the vicinity of caves and rock art. Yet they neither paint on the rocks nor sleep in the caves although they sometimes take refuge there from the midday sun (147). They say that the exquisite paintings that adorn the hills (148) must always have been there, because the 'old people' could not say who the artists were.

Several hundred kilometres to the west, on the edge of the Namib Desert, a fine hunting study (149) fades on a rock wall that has not echoed the sound of Bushman voices for at least half a century.

147

148

149

Previous page: Startled by the sound of an engine, wildebeest thunder across the savanna in the central Kalahari.

The apparent monotony of the Kalahari belies the variety of its wildlife: a bat-eared fox (151), its ears laid back, senses danger; a young kudu bull (152) browses on berries, and Khu stalks a gemsbok (153). Still 200 metres from his quarry, Khu bends low, but when he makes his final approach he will drop to his elbows and knees.

Bushman and black-maned Kalahari lion compete as predators for the antelope. Sometimes they track the same animal, and their spoor lies side by side (154).

154   155

Filling the stomachs of the band is a daily chore, for the Kalahari seldom provides a surplus. But the Bushman, as he moves about the land he knows and understands so well, is able to draw upon a surprisingly wide although erratic range of foods. The warthog (156) hides in its burrow from predators, but the Bushman, superpredator, spears him from above. Likewise the yellow-billed hornbill and her chicks (157) are protected in their clay-sealed hollow in a tree. There they are safe from most enemies. If the seal is broken, the hen withdraws into a narrow chimney above her nest and hides there. But the Bushmen, knowing her secret, reach in and pull her out, heedless of her loud protest.

In lean times, even the python does not escape the hunter's spear (158). As for the tortoise (159), it is ignominiously fitted with a bark handle and carried back to camp alive to be roasted in its shell.

These decorations and adornments reflect the Bushman's flair and ability to adapt new materials such as glass and plastic trade beads for an ancient aesthetic purpose (160, 161 & 162). Their hand-wrought rawhide sandals (163) do not divorce them from the earth.

When a honeyguide (164) was seen at the N/ausha camp one morning, several people set off after it. Whenever it stopped, Bo went forward and spoke to it (165). The bird led them to a hive in a dead tamboti tree where the Bushmen subdued the bees with smoke (166), felled the tree and then broke open the hive (167). Then everyone indulged in the Bushman passion for honey.

164

165

Previous page: At the end of the dry season it is common to see bushfires scorching the veld. To attract game, the Bushmen set fire to the dry grass, which encourages new growth when the first rains fall.

Twilight comes to the village of a Bushman band which has built its huts in the style of black people and adopted the trappings of alien cultures (170).
An international boundary fence between Botswana and Namibia now dissects the ancient hunting grounds of the Bushmen, but stiles (171) have been erected over which they alone may pass at will, without passports.

Overleaf: This woman has seen the passing of a way of life. Already her grandchildren belong to a world in which her values and her culture have no place.